SOMETHING'S GOTTA CHANGE

REDEFINING COLLABORATIVE LINGUISTIC RESEARCH

SOMETHING'S GOTTA CHANGE
REDEFINING COLLABORATIVE LINGUISTIC RESEARCH

LESLEY WOODS

ANU PRESS

ASIA-PACIFIC LINGUISTICS

This book is dedicated to my mentor Jeannie Bell. Jeannie has been a long-term champion for the human rights of Indigenous people in linguistic research.

ANU PRESS

Published by ANU Press
The Australian National University
Canberra ACT 2600, Australia
Email: anupress@anu.edu.au

Available to download for free at press.anu.edu.au

ISBN (print): 9781760465476
ISBN (online): 9781760465483

WorldCat (print): 1370915771
WorldCat (online): 1370987666

DOI: 10.22459/SGC.2022

This title is published under a Creative Commons Attribution-NonCommercial-NoDerivatives 4.0 International (CC BY-NC-ND 4.0) licence.

The full licence terms are available at creativecommons.org/licenses/by-nc-nd/4.0/legalcode

Cover design and layout by ANU Press. Cover photograph by Stephen Dent.

This book is published under the aegis of the Asia-Pacific Linguistics editorial board of ANU Press.

This edition © 2023 ANU Press

Contents

Abstract	ix
List of abbreviations	xi
1. Introduction	**1**
2. What do we already know?	**7**
2.1 Community language and cultural heritage rights	7
2.2 Raising awareness within communities	16
2.3 Motivation for language work	19
2.4 Non-Indigenous linguists: Documentation of endangered languages	20
2.5 Indigenous communities: Language maintenance and revival	22
2.6 Participating in the project of decolonisation	26
2.7 Specialist training	30
2.8 Guidelines, protocols and linguists' field guides	33
2.9 Funding for linguistic research and language projects	38
2.10 Decolonising linguistics	43
3. The research project	**47**
3.1 Why did I want to do this research?	47
3.2 How did I do it?	47
3.3 Who did I talk to?	49
4. What did they say?	**53**
4.1 Indigenous control of language and cultural knowledge	53
4.2 Copyright, intellectual property rights and agreements	62
4.3 Community directed research: Identifying communities' research needs	80
4.4 The issues and moving forward together	90
4.5 Creating opportunities for discussion: A way forward	106
5. Where to now?	**115**
5.1. The publish or perish dilemma: Secondary uses of research data	115
5.2 Indigenous control of research and use of agreements	117

5.3 Indigenous linguistic training and work	118
5.4 Community education of the issues	118
5.5 Co-authoring	119
5.6 Shared goals	120
5.7 Research funding	122
5.8 Appropriate training for non-Indigenous linguists	123
5.9 A new direction for collaboration	124

References 127

Abstract

The current models of ethical linguistic research in Australia have reached a crossroads, with Indigenous communities beginning to reject linguistic research and documentation of their languages in some areas around Australia, and many Indigenous organisations becoming anti-linguist entirely. In this book, I investigate what has gone wrong and what can be done to bring linguistic practice and research into line with Indigenous peoples' desires and expectations in the field. The notion that non-Indigenous linguists and Indigenous people and communities share the same goals to save their highly endangered languages is not valid if 'saving' the language, to the non-Indigenous linguist, means writing a grammar or producing a dictionary before the last speakers die. Indigenous people are saying they want their languages to be passed on 'breath to breath' from parent to child or speaker to language learner, so they do not 'go to sleep' and they want their sleeping languages back on their tongues. They want their languages to be a part of their future, not their past. They want control over their languages and cultural knowledge. The search for new knowledge and the 'publish or perish' mentality of academia and copyright laws serve to take Indigenous peoples' language and knowledge away from Indigenous people and communities and pass it over to the global scientific community. Indigenous people want to be in control of knowledge production that concerns us, or is about us, and we have begun to participate in producing our own knowledge about ourselves for ourselves and the global scientific community. What we are seeing is Indigenous people pushing back against being the 'subjects of scientific research' and therefore we are now at a crossroads. This research examines the issues and seeks to find practical solutions, from both Indigenous and non-Indigenous perspectives, to the ethical dilemmas in developing linguistic research practice that meets the needs of Indigenous people and communities, and non-Indigenous linguists. It fleshes out and redefines the concept of genuinely collaborative and ethical linguistic research and work with Indigenous people and communities and has applications beyond linguistics.

List of abbreviations

AIATSIS	Australian Institute of Aboriginal and Torres Strait Islander Studies
ALS	Australian Linguistic Society
ARC	Australian Research Council
BIITE	Batchelor Institute for Indigenous Tertiary Education
CoEDL	ARC Centre of Excellence for the Dynamics of Language
DRIL	Documenting and Revitalising Indigenous Languages (program)
ICIP	Indigenous Cultural and Intellectual Property
KLRC	Kimberley Language Resource Centre
RNLD	Resource Network for Linguistic Diversity
SAL	School of Australian Linguistics
VACL	Victorian Aboriginal Corporation for Languages

1

Introduction

> There is a need to educate the public, as well as scientific and academic associations, to respect the rights of Indigenous peoples to privacy, cultural integrity and control of their own heritage through their own laws and institutions.
>
> Erica Irene Daes, 1993

Central to the issues explored in this book are two main themes: these are the right of Indigenous peoples to have complete control of their heritage languages and cultural knowledges, and the false distinction made by the global scientific community between intellectual property rights and copyright. Special rapporteur, Erica Irene Daes, in her report to the United Nations Sub-Commission on the Prevention of Discrimination and Protection of Minorities (1993, pp. 8–9) concluded that from Indigenous people's point of view, there is no distinction between cultural and intellectual property and the global scientific community's distinctions in this regard are artificial. Daes states:

> Indigenous peoples regard all products of the human mind and heart as interrelated, and as flowing from the same source: the relationships between the people and their land, their kinship with the other living creatures that share the land, and with the spirit world.

Across countries that English speakers invaded such as Canada, the USA, New Zealand and Australia we are seeing Indigenous peoples pushing back against research and asserting their rights to have control over their languages and cultural knowledge. Increasingly, this is being seen as a matter of basic human rights. The huge disparity between Indigenous peoples' realities and responsibilities around their relationships to their cultural knowledge, which is embedded in their languages, and the non-Indigenous systems of copyright and intellectual property rights, is at the heart of the widening gap between the practices of research in the academy and Indigenous communities. As custodians of their traditional knowledge, Indigenous peoples' concepts of and responsibilities for managing this knowledge are in direct conflict with the system of copyright and the practice of linguistic research conducted by non-Indigenous linguists and, more broadly, research in any field that involves Indigenous people.

The current model of ethical linguistic research in Indigenous communities in the Australian context fails to address these issues, because there is a general reluctance by non-Indigenous linguists to let go of control over their research and projects for fear of how this will impact their careers and work practices, particularly for linguists working as academics. Also, non-Indigenous linguists and other academics have been used to the idea that they should be free to pursue their interests regardless of what other people think, including the speakers of Indigenous languages. Australian Indigenous people are asserting their rights to maintain control of their languages and cultural knowledge, and we are now at a crossroads. We are in need of a new model of ethical linguistic research that aims to address issues of human rights, which the now outdated models of linguistic research have until now failed to address.

To date, in the field of linguistics in Australia, these issues have not been proactively addressed because it is seen as too political and too sensitive—there is so much at stake on both sides—and the problem is often assigned to the 'too-hard' basket. Sometimes at gatherings where Indigenous linguists, activists, language workers and non-Indigenous linguists come together, tensions overflow and everyone is left feeling either frustrated, angry or under attack because there has been no space made for discussion or resolution of the issues between the parties, and the issues seem to get pushed even further down.

However, there are some non-Indigenous linguists who are very dedicated to seeing reform in linguistic research and practice and they partner willingly with Indigenous people and communities to address the issues on the ground. These dedicated and brave linguists are the champions of ethical linguistic practice and walk with Indigenous people on this journey.

There is a growing anti-linguist sentiment in Indigenous communities precisely because these issues have not been adequately addressed. It is not enough to have a static statement or policy on ethics that never gets acted upon or continually reviewed to keep up with current trends. This is seeing Indigenous communities and organisations beginning to reject linguistic research in their areas and aspiring to get the skills to do their own linguistic work. As an Indigenous linguist, I believe that Indigenous people gaining linguistic skills and undertaking their own language work is imperative in order to ensure that Indigenous people themselves will be able to manage and control their languages and cultural knowledge according to traditional practice in their areas. Non-Indigenous linguists worry what this will mean for their work practices and careers, particularly if they work as academics in university settings and they wonder: if our agendas are not the same, will we still have a working relationship?

However, Indigenous people need the help of non-Indigenous linguists; there is too much work that urgently needs to be done. The Indigenous languages that have not already gone to sleep are in various stages of serious endangerment, many critically endangered. The languages that have gone to sleep need to be reclaimed and spoken again. Indigenous people need non-Indigenous linguists to help Indigenous people and communities do this work, and this is beginning to be seen as an important motivation and a valid role by many non-Indigenous linguists. Indigenous people need to continue working with non-Indigenous linguists in ways that address the human rights concerns of Indigenous people and communities.

This research explores the issues in depth both from an Indigenous perspective and a non-Indigenous perspective and asks the question:

> How best can non-Indigenous researchers, in the fields of applied and documentary linguistics, work collaboratively with Indigenous communities to achieve research outcomes that are in the best interests of, and for the benefit of, both the community and the researcher?

As already mentioned, many non-Indigenous linguists are working hard to find constructive solutions to help address the issues and concerns of Indigenous people around ethics in linguistic research. There is a genuine desire to see urgent reforms in the linguistic research framework, in ways that would give agency to Indigenous people and to develop genuinely ethical collaborative working relationships.

There is also consensus on both sides that there is an urgent need to have a forum where non-Indigenous linguists and Indigenous linguists and practitioners can come together and have open, robust discussions about the issues and work out a way forward as a collective.

Practical strategies discussed in this book include the implementation of agreements and licensing to use language and cultural materials that see Indigenous people retain and maintain control over their cultural knowledge, and co-authoring publications and possibly dissertations. Other issues discussed in this book are ethics applications and agreements within the academy and what constitutes a co-researcher and co-analyst of language data.

The research in this publication is qualitative in nature and is based on Indigenous research methodologies and perspectives; in this way, this book is presented in plain English and in a semi-narrative format, including my own voice. The target audience for this book is both Indigenous people and non-Indigenous linguists; however, I believe this research would also be of value to researchers in other fields who are engaging with Indigenous people.

I conducted interviews with three Indigenous linguists and language activists and three non-Indigenous linguists, who I would consider to be activists for Indigenous people and their languages. I chose these particular people because I wanted to draw from their shared experiences, honest opinions and practical solutions to show some of the very difficult dilemmas we now face in the discipline.

The aim of this book is to flesh out the issues identified in the previous pages and find a path towards developing a genuinely ethical and collaborative linguistic research framework that addresses the issues and concerns of both parties.

Chapter 2 looks at what we already know from the relevant literature. I found a huge volume of literature around the subject of ethics in research more broadly, both from an Indigenous and a non-Indigenous perspective. The topic of ethical research in linguistics has been another matter; many non-Indigenous linguists have written on the topic, but I was able to find only a couple of published papers by Indigenous linguists in the Australian context.

Critically, then, this book provides a desperately needed contribution to the literature that encompasses both Indigenous and non-Indigenous voices on the issues of ethics in linguistic research in the Australian context. It provides unique insights from both sides and lays the foundations for further research and for opportunities to further discussions between the parties.

Chapter 3 gives some background information about the people who participated in the research and the reasoning behind the choices I made about how to present the outcomes of the research.

Chapter 4 provides an in-depth look at the discussions around the issues and includes my own views on some of the topics. This chapter is divided into four main topic areas; there is some overlap in the topics, but it is considered important to discuss each separately.

Chapter 5 provides a summary of the major findings and outcomes from the research and recommendations for further discussion and research.

2
What do we already know?

2.1 Community language and cultural heritage rights

> As discussions develop regarding the principles and ethics governing Indigenous research, the issue of control or decision making reverberates the singular most important principle—Indigenous peoples must control their own knowledge, a custodial ownership that prescribes from the customs, rules, and practices of each group.
> Marie Battiste (2008, p. 501)

Many Indigenous scholars and activists are beginning to articulate the need for Indigenous peoples to become more active in and aware of the impacts of research that is conducted within, or that concerns, their communities, and their knowledges. In response to this growing concern and awareness, Indigenous communities are developing new ethics and protocols for working with Indigenous people and these are beginning to be implemented by major funding organisations around the world such as the Endangered Languages Documentation Programme.[1]

In the field of linguistics, many non-Indigenous linguists are beginning to come to terms with what this means for them and the ways they work with Indigenous communities now and into the future. Indigenous people

---

1 www.eldp.net/en/our+grants/documentation+grants/

and communities are also working through the issues of how to engage with non-Indigenous linguists in ways that meet their needs to ensure the protection of their cultural knowledges and self-determination.

However, in the Australian context, we are still very much at the beginning of the process of teasing out the issues and finding our way forward, with language and cultural rights being high on the agenda as one of the most important issues for Indigenous peoples.

My experience as an Indigenous linguist suggests that there is sufficient goodwill between Indigenous communities and non-Indigenous linguists who share, for the most part, common goals, and that the issues are beginning to be worked through and solutions found. Working relationships between Indigenous people and non-Indigenous linguists aim to be far more equitable than they have been in the past and they aim to address the issues of human rights and equality in linguistic research.

Indigenous linguist Jeannie Bell asks the question: 'Who makes decisions about community rights?' (2010). She points out that endorsed community language representatives and tribal Elders demanded to be consulted and involved in any discussions around matters relating to research about them at an Indigenous languages conference in 2007. She goes on to say that Indigenous delegates of the conference stated strongly that they must have more control in research that concerns Indigenous people, regardless of whether the research is historical or contemporary. As Indigenous people become more aware and empowered, they are beginning to take control of their language and cultural heritage. At times, the Indigenous community's aspirations and goals can be in conflict with those of non-Indigenous linguists. This can lead to communities not allowing access to their language for ongoing linguistic documentation (Hinton, 2010; Hobson et al., 2010; Newry & Palmer, 2003; Olawsky, 2010).

There are many parallels between Indigenous communities around the world in our struggles to gain holistic recognition and respect for the control and management of our knowledges because the issues are broadly similar in many respects. Indigenous people in many parts of the world and, more recently in Australia, are now calling for research that supports and contributes to their struggles for self-determination as defined and controlled by their own communities (Rigney, 1999, p. 110). Rigney points out that non-Indigenous people have long been at the helm of knowledge production, including extraction, storage and control of knowledge about Indigenous peoples, and that this knowledge and the ownership of this knowledge has been the basis of many academic qualifications and careers. Chickasaw linguist and anthropologist Jenny Davis says (2017, p. 40):

> This literal and metaphorical extraction from context is itself a colonial enterprise and often a cornerstone of Western science—one that removes people from homelands, loots objects from graves in the name of science and education and disassociates products from those who labour to produce them. In other words, it celebrates the empire in empirical.

Illustrating Davis's point about the colonial enterprise of science is the debate in Australia about the re-burial of the human remains of Mungo Man and Mungo Lady, who were removed from the Willandra Lakes region in New South Wales in 1974 and 1968, respectively, along with many other human remains (Daley, 2021; Westerway et al., 2021). Daley reports that the geologist Jim Bowler, who removed the remains, asserts that the remains should not be reburied and claims that reburial would diminish the World Heritage values of the Willandra Lakes region.

Westerway et al. (2021) report that many scientists' voices have been overlooked and that the remains should continue to be available for scientific research such as helping to develop an understanding of how people adapted to climate change. While debate continues amongst some of the traditional owner groups, Paakantji, Mutthi Mutthi and Ngiyampaa, the representative Elders of each group and the chair of the Aboriginal advisory group want the remains to be reburied. They believe that 'their spirits will not rest until they are reinterred, one way or another, in country' and that Bowler should 'stop interfering, he's had his time'. This example is a poignant reminder that Western research seeks to be privileged, in this case over the authority and wishes of Indigenous Elders, who have many thousands of years of collective cultural and spiritual knowledge.

The final decision rested with the federal minister for the environment and, after a period of seeking public feedback and further consultation, the minister agreed to reburial.[2]

---

2   www.theguardian.com/australia-news/2022/apr/25/were-talking-about-2000-generations-mungo-man-and-mungo-lady-reburial-divides-traditional-owners

In light of the continuing practice of privileging the colonial framework for research, Rigney rightly states that it is no surprise that Indigenous people are apprehensive and cautious with regard to research that is about or concerns Indigenous people and knowledge in general. However, he makes the point, and I agree, that this does not mean that Indigenous people reject research outright, and he highlights the fact that some research by non-Indigenous people has been beneficial to the project of self-determination (1999, p. 109).

Indigenous knowledge and voices must hold in matters that concern Indigenous people. Mi'kmaq author, educator and professor emerita at the University of Saskatchewan Marie Battiste says that, in the absence of protection for Indigenous knowledge in national and international laws, Indigenous peoples and communities must now develop their own processes (2008, p. 506). She states that the role of representatives responsible for the holding and passing down of knowledge, and the inclusion of the Indigenous community voice, are central to arriving at solutions to the issues of control of research being conducted among or about Indigenous peoples. One very good example of Indigenous community control is given by Racquel-Maria Yamada, who says that the Kari'nja community leaders were adamant about maintaining control over language and cultural materials in their local archive in her work in South America (2007, p. 270).

The notion of restricting access to language and cultural information does not sit comfortably with liberal thinkers in Western democracies but the restriction of knowledge is common in Aboriginal societies (Newry & Palmer, 2003, p. 103). Newry and Palmer state that within Miriwoong culture, restriction of access to knowledge is associated with age, gender, and status and is embedded in the cultural norms surrounding a death or marriage in the community. It was within these cultural practices and norms that, in 2003, the Miriwoong people from the Kununurra region of Western Australia were no longer willing to distribute language and cultural materials to the open market where control was then out of their hands. They point out that this approach was taken to prevent inappropriate and/or incorrect use of the language and a possible breach of strict social protocols (2003, p. 105), and, importantly, that it enabled their limited resources to be utilised specifically for ensuring future generations of Miriwoong retain and increase the use of their language and cultural knowledge.

Knut Olawsky points out that protectionism is completely understandable from a historical point of view when, in the case of the Miriwoong, as is with many other language groups across Australia, language or language materials are often the last thing left, that has not been taken away, and that Indigenous people might exercise any control over (2010, p. 78). Reclaiming authority over language and language work is part of a much bigger project of reclaiming sovereignty and self-determination (Eira, 2007, p. 83). Indigenous authority in this regard means reclaiming the right to exercise control over all aspects of language and cultural knowledge and what does or does not happen to that knowledge in a given context, particularly in the context of research by institutions such as universities, government and non-government organisations.

The Miriwoong people later on relaxed their policies around the restriction of language and cultural materials. Their language centre now has a policy of 'language publicity' (Olawsky, 2010, pp. 77–78). Olawsky says that this strategy is aimed at supporting the revitalisation efforts of Miriwoong in the broader community, including having the language recognised as the legitimate traditional language of the area. However, this approach is still very much controlled by the traditional authorities and the priority is still to support and implement language maintenance and learning for the Miriwoong community. It is worth noting that once the Miriwoong people's concerns about control of language and cultural knowledge were managed by the community, the Miriwoong people were more open to sharing aspects of their knowledge in a controlled manner. In 2017, the Mirima Dawang Woorlab-gerring language centre published *Miriwoong Woorlang Yawoorroonga-woorr*, the first ever public dictionary in the Miriwoong language.[3]

The growing urgency of Indigenous people to regain control over their language and cultural knowledge, combined with the distrust of the global scientific community, sees Indigenous peoples increasingly looking to conduct their own research. Rigney (1999) examines the impact that research has traditionally had on Indigenous peoples and he discusses the role that Indigenous people have to play in conducting their own research for the project of liberation and self-determination. While Rigney acknowledges that the critical research by non-Indigenous people that seeks to inform the struggles of Indigenous people must continue and

---

3   mirima.org.au/a-miriwoong-lexicon-for-all/

is welcome, he points out that research by Indigenous people goes to the heart of Indigenous people's struggles and, importantly, he says Indigenous researchers are accountable to their communities (1999, p. 117).

The Kimberley Language Resource Centre (KLRC) made tentative steps towards the goal of self-determination (KLRC 2010), which saw its Board of Directors decide to change the organisation's strategic direction to concentrate its focus on oral transmission of languages. This move drew criticism from non-Indigenous linguists who argued that the linguistic community and the broader Indigenous community are being let down because documentation is not being encouraged (2010, p. 141). The KLRC Board asserted that Aboriginal people want and need to be actively involved in the decisions that affect the survival of their languages. They were concerned about what impact this criticism might have at the level of policy development and funding programs. The board pointed out that linguists' opinions inform government and their lack of support for the community's authority in this regard could potentially have a negative effect on the development of policies about language funding priorities, which could otherwise be supportive of the language maintenance strategies that the KLRC have undertaken to prioritise.

The KLRC also questioned why some non-Indigenous linguists seemingly dismiss or refuse to acknowledge the views and authority of the community and their nominated representatives (2010, pp. 142–143). They ask:

> Does lack of understanding or disagreement on the part of the non-Aboriginal person make Aboriginal decisions about languages wrong? [and]

> Why are Aboriginal continuation strategies seen as less valid than the strategies of Western academia and education?

The KLRC's questions are valid and are in accordance with Battiste's criticism, that is, that Eurocentric colonisers have considered themselves to be the superior culture and an ideal model for humanity, and therefore believe that they can then assess the competencies of others (Battiste 2008, p. 504). The KLRC sought to have the voices of the communities it represents heard and supported despite having to struggle with the top-down approach from governments and the imposed academic approach of the non-Indigenous linguistic community (KLRC 2010, p. 143). They say:

> We have to ask not only 'whose languages?' but 'whose language centre is it anyway?'

Prominent Australian linguists Simon Musgrave and Nick Thieberger question the degree of control that Indigenous communities can exercise and are critical of language centres that have chosen to restrict documentation in their areas, despite there being no formal structure that provides them with the authority to stop research (2007, p. 50). It is not clear from their discussion what constitutes the formal structure mentioned in their paper or why they question the authority of the elected representatives of the community, who are vested with the responsibility to act on behalf of and for the benefit of the community as a whole.

Rigney (2001) critiques the origins of what he refers to as Western scientific rationalisation and the role that Indigenous Australians now play in the academy. He states that although the authority of Western science is no longer unquestioned, the notion persists that Western constructed science is authoritative, neutral, universal and privileges itself, and it can therefore be used as the yardstick against which all other realities are measured and judged 'rational' or otherwise (2001, p. 3). He says of Indigenous scholars, and I would include here any Indigenous person or organisation who challenges the authority of global scientific research (2001, pp. 4–5):

> Indigenous scholars have always had to justify not only our humanness and our Aboriginality, but also the fact that our intellects are 'rational' and that we have the right to take our legitimate place in the academy of research.

Rigney says that the logical conclusion of privileging Western science in this way would be that scientific methods and knowledge production used by other cultures would be viewed as inferior and irrational (Rigney, 2001, p. 4). Further, Richard Grounds, the director of the Euchee/Yuchi language project (Oklahoma) and member of the Yuchi nation says (Grounds 2021, p. 61):

> When the institutions that grow out of a colonial system of 'civilization' are generally understood to represent fairness, the voice of reason, and notions such as scientific detachment, it becomes difficult to shape a critique from an Indigenous perspective that does not sound shrill, unreasonable, and overly judgmental.

Rigney and other Australian Indigenous scholars and linguists—and, in some cases, their non-Indigenous co-authors, such as Bell (2010), Couzens et al. (2020), Fesl (1993), Gaby & Woods (2020) and Riley (2021)—and Indigenous linguists and scholars from other countries (e.g. Charity Hudley et al. 2019; Czaykowska-Higgins, 2009; Davis, 2017; Grounds, 2021; Leonard, 2017, 2021; Smith, 2021; Wilson, 2008) are questioning the status quo and challenging the colonial practices of the academy. They are now developing what is known broadly as Indigenist research methodologies, which aim to promote progressive approaches to Indigenous knowledge production. Indigenist research methodologies are becoming so well recognised that there are now several important publications, such as the *Handbook of Critical Indigenous Methodologies* (Densin et al., 2008) and *The Routledge Handbook of Critical Indigenous Studies* (Hokowhitu et al., 2020). This research framework seeks to overcome epistemic violence against Indigenous peoples caused by being subject to research by non-Indigenous researchers, and it frames research around Indigenous people's own priorities and interests rather than the priorities and interests of non-Indigenous researchers.

In writing about Western research in the Orient, Palestinian American author Edward Said stated that it was his hope that colonised peoples would not take up the formidable discourse of Western culture and apply this to themselves and others in their own research (1994, p. 25). Rigney agrees and asserts that the challenge for Indigenism is to resist and overcome the opposites in Western scientific thought (2001, p. 7):

> Western scientific epistemologies, ethics and meta-theories are not only racialised but also sexist and classist. Indigenism must overcome the dichotomies in scientific thought such as object/subject, rational/irrational and white/black. Indigenism is now asking: 'can we participate in Western science without reinventing the hegemonic colonial imagination about ourselves?'

Māori educationist Linda Tuhiwai Smith says (2005, p. 87) that the majority of global research in the fields of social sciences conducted by non-Indigenous researchers is seen predominantly as a tool of colonisation and as having limited application in assisting Indigenous people with the project of self-determination and development.

Indigenous people should control their own knowledge and do their own research and this should be at the heart of the principles for research policy and practice (Battiste, 2008, p. 502). Importantly, Battiste says that if non-Indigenous researchers want to enter into a collaborative research relationship with Indigenous peoples, such research should empower and benefit Indigenous communities, not just researchers, their educational institutions or broader society. American linguist and professor emerita of linguistics at the University of California at Berkeley Leanne Hinton gives the initiatives of the Volkswagen Foundation, the Program of Documentation of Endangered Languages project,[4] as an example of the current trends of strong representation of community interests, and points out that these trends are driven by the communities themselves and their language activists (Hinton, 2010, p. 36). Hinton is also director emerita of the Survey of California and Other Indian Languages, and participates in language revitalisation efforts and organisations, including the Advocates for Indigenous California Language Survival and its biennial Breath of Life conferences.[5] Importantly, Hinton says that community control of languages may not be a goal that non-Indigenous linguists think about in particular but it is often the goal of community members and can broadly have the following meanings (Hinton, 2010, p. 40):

1. Community access to or possession of original or copies of field notes, recordings, and documents on the language.
2. Communities doing their own documentation of their language rather than relying on outside linguists.
3. Communities working with linguists on community terms, control of who works with the language, and what they do, often involving contracts or retainers of linguistic services.
4. Community members acquiring an education in linguistics or language education.
5. Communities being in charge of their own language programs and their own schools.

Hinton goes on to say that issues around community control can raise possible points of conflict with the non-Indigenous linguist around intellectual property rights of documentation, and around who may or may not have access to language materials that are products of the research project. This is a trend that we are beginning to see in the Australian context also and this is evidenced in the discussions of this research presented in Chapter 4.

---

4   www.volkswagenstiftung.de
5   en.wikipedia.org/wiki/Leanne_Hinton

2.2 Raising awareness within communities

While Indigenous activists and scholars in Australia are becoming aware of the issues around ethics in linguistic research and research more broadly, many Indigenous people in remote and rural areas who do not have a representative organisation, such as a language centre, are vulnerable to the impacts of research and the protection of their cultural knowledges into the future. Richard Grounds points out that when an Indigenous community has no organisation that speaks on its behalf, the community remains vulnerable. He says (2007):[6]

> Within the Yuchi community, our struggle with these questions reached a peak with the request of a linguist to develop a dictionary for the Yuchi language. The formal proposal had already been submitted to the appropriate governmental agency, and a meeting was convened after the fact for approval by the community. In our community, like most small language communities, there was no institutional review board to take up such questions or look after the interests of the community in the context of academic research.

Without strong and robust representation, the idea that free, prior and informed consent would address the issues of copyright, control of language and cultural knowledge and representation in research is yet to be realised in a concrete way. What does free, prior and informed consent look like? The UN Manual for National Human Rights Institutions (APFNHRI & OHCHR, 2013, p. 28) outlines the following:

> Free implies that there is no coercion, intimidation, or manipulation.
>
> Prior implies that consent is to be sought sufficiently in advance of any authorization or commencement of activities and respect is shown to time requirements of indigenous consultation/consensus processes.
>
> Informed implies that information is provided that covers a range of aspects, including the nature, size, pace, reversibility and scope of any proposed project or activity; the purpose of the project as well as its duration; locality and areas affected; a preliminary assessment of the likely economic, social, cultural, and environmental impact, including potential risks; personnel likely to be involved in the execution of the project; and procedures

---

6   www.culturalsurvival.org

the project may entail. This process may include the option of withholding consent. Consultation and participation are crucial components of a consent process.

Indigenous people around the world are increasingly becoming aware of the political issues that face them in relation to the protection of their Indigenous knowledge (Battiste, 2008, p. 506). However, Battiste points out that at the level of the local community, there is still a need to bring communities up to speed on the issues and that communities must become aware and educated to gain a holistic understanding of the issues, practices and protocols for doing research. Communities must decide on processes that ensure that principles of protection and use of knowledge are developed, shared widely and become the normal standards for research within their communities and territories, lest they continue to be vulnerable to the threats to their cultures, knowledges and communities by virtue of research being done on them (2008, p. 502). In Australia, there are huge gaps in Indigenous people's awareness of the issues at the community level in many regional and remote areas. Many Indigenous people would struggle to understand exactly what free, prior and informed consent even is or why it is important in the research context.

Does lack of awareness of the deeper issues within communities create obstacles in forming truly collaborative and productive research projects?

Musgrave and Thieberger say that while collaborative research with community members is ideal, it can be problematic and of limited value. They offer examples from their own research experiences and outline the lack of community engagement. They say that the idea of research 'for' let alone 'by' a community presupposes that at least some members of a community are willing to engage in the research project in order to influence the research agenda, and they say that the community may 'accept' or 'tolerate' the research project but may not be sufficiently interested to provide direction (2007, p. 47). Further, they point out that the onerous ethics and protocol requirements of funding bodies, such as providing funding on the condition of proof of community support, may be a factor in a community's lack of engagement in research (2007, p. 49). Dutch linguist George van Driem agrees and says that introducing ethics and protocols sows the seeds of distrust and potentially spoils the relationship between the researcher and language informants (van Driem, 2016, p. 244).

Are the problems identified above a result of the lack of a grounded understanding of the issues and an active engagement in 'planning' and 'setting of the agenda' of research projects? Did these communities initiate or request the research from an identified need? In relation to the lack of interest noted by Musgrave and Thieberger, is it possible to propose here that this could be attributed to a kind of informal revolt in the form of inertia, a confused and vague reaction against the colonisers (Williams, 1983, pp. 334–335). Referring to the oppressed labour forces in Great Britain between the eighteenth and twentieth centuries, Williams points out that, all too often, withdrawal of interest is interpreted as proving the unfitness of the communities concerned. Williams states that inertia and apathy have always been employed by the governed as a comparatively safe weapon against their governors (1983, p. 335).

If non-Indigenous linguists and Indigenous communities can approach research as a shared venture, recognising that each in different ways may need the other, there will be no need for fear or defensiveness on either side. Canadian linguist at the University of Toronto Keren Rice aptly says (2009, p. 56):

> I began this paper by suggesting that there might be two solitudes, dividing linguists and language activists. Must there be two solitudes? The answer to this is maybe not, if there is mutual recognition that a linguist cannot on their own save a language; it takes a community of people to do that. In order to truly work together, general principles such as relationships, respect, reciprocity and recognition are critical.

There has been fear and defensiveness on both sides and for very different reasons. For Indigenous people it has been and continues to be the need to maintain or regain control over their languages and cultural knowledges in line with human rights conventions. For non-Indigenous linguists it is the fear of letting go of control over research and how this might impact their careers; some resentment at the idea of not having the unimpeded freedom to explore the questions they'd like to explore might also be present.

In Section 2.9 we will take a closer look at the how the funding models currently impact both of these factors.

2.3 Motivation for language work

There is a growing urgency among Indigenous communities to keep their languages alive and viable through language maintenance and oral continuation, or to breathe life back into them through revitalisation programs. This is demonstrated by numerous language projects and programs to be found across Australia. Many of these emanate from language centres where it might be assumed that there is some level of local Indigenous control and ownership of programs and the resulting language materials produced. Most language centres have an all-Indigenous board of management, but this may not equate to having total control of operations and projects. Often non-Indigenous staff and linguists are at the helm of management and language projects. This can sometimes be a barrier to meeting the communities' directives and expectations for language maintenance or revitalisation and for being self-determining.

Many articles have been written that describe language revitalisation and maintenance efforts in Australia; for just a few, see various chapters in the edited collection *Reawakening Languages: Theory and Practice in the Revitalisation of Australia's Indigenous Languages* (Hobson et al., 2010) and more recently discussions around Indigenous language education in schools (Angelo & Poetsch, 2019; Poetsch et al., 2019). For examples of local language revitalisation efforts in other countries see Hinton (2013) and Hinton & Hale (2001) and numerous papers in the proceedings of the Foundation for Endangered Languages annual conferences.[7]

However, these types of programs, while incredibly important and central to Indigenous communities, are not the focus of this book. It is the role of universities and the currently accepted model of linguistic research, including language documentation, that is the focus of this volume.

Shawn Wilson, an Opaskwayak Cree from northern Manitoba in Canada, says that research is all about unanswered questions (Wilson, 2008, p. 6). Linguistic research then seeks to answer questions about aspects of how a language works, such as word and sentence structure (the grammar) and word and sentence meaning (semantics). It can ask questions about ancient writing systems and historical accounts of sleeping languages. Linguistic research can also ask questions about the way sounds are made

---

7   www.ogmios.org/conferences/

in the mouth (phonetics), sound systems of a language (phonology), language learning or acquisition and disorders of communication and much more. Questions around 'how a language is structured' (grammar and semantics) are the focus of language documentation projects.

Some Indigenous communities have been involved in language documentation projects for many decades and are beginning to question if documentation alone will save their languages. They are increasingly choosing to take control of their language programs in an effort to reverse the rapid decline in the number of people speaking the languages and to regain and maintain control of their language and cultural knowledge.

This move has some non-Indigenous linguists concerned that language documentation will take a back seat within communities. They argue that documentation efforts in the past have provided communities whose languages are severely endangered, or which have gone to sleep, with valuable materials for language revitalisation and reclamation projects. Non-Indigenous linguists also argue for the right to continue to pursue their interests and contribute to the scientific understanding of languages in the global field of linguistics.

We are beginning to witness a widening gap in the goals of Indigenous communities and non-Indigenous linguists. Some Indigenous communities are beginning to reject documentary and other kinds of linguistic research that concerns them more broadly.

2.4 Non-Indigenous linguists: Documentation of endangered languages

The non-Indigenous linguist's motivation to undertake linguistic research or fieldwork in Indigenous communities may come either from a genuine desire or commitment to documenting endangered languages and global language diversity and/or be the result of a request from a community where an ongoing relationship exists between the linguist and the community (Bell, 2010, p. 89). Bell says that quite often this research is a requirement of the linguist's academic institution; a requisite for attaining their qualifications. She goes on to say that for the majority of non-Indigenous linguists, an interest in Australian languages is motivated by the universals of language, such as the grammatical, semantic or typological features of the languages, and the contribution the linguist can make to the scientific literature for future generations of the global scientific community. Musgrave and Thieberger (2007, p. 49) agree and say that, traditionally, university-based linguists are generally concerned with issues of interest to the broader field of linguistics and/or in documenting a record of the grammar of a language. They go on to say that a part of the motivation for linguistic research is to broaden linguists' understanding of universal linguistic typologies. Musgrave and Thieberger say that the work associated with what they term 'language affection', that is the production of language teaching resources associated with language revitalisation, is, for many linguists, 'thin and unsatisfying'.

Giving something back to the Indigenous community is a genuine desire shared by many linguists (Bell, 2010, p. 89). Hinton agrees and points out that there has been a shift from preservation of linguistic diversity for future generations of linguists, to understanding the potential of documentation to future generations of community members. Importantly, she points out that this was usually the motivation of the community people who agreed to work with the linguist in the first place (2010, p. 37). She says that communities whose languages today are 'sleeping' make very good use of previous documentation efforts in revitalising their languages, and this is further incentive for linguists to undertake language documentation that will meet the future needs of the community. In this respect, Hinton talks about documentation projects that include recording conversational language that will be of critical importance to community members in the future as second language learners. In many cases, past documentation efforts have resulted in the creation of much of the recorded material available for some languages as rightly noted by Musgrave and Thieberger (2007, p. 49).

However, giving back to communities that have been involved in linguistic research involves much more than handing back a manuscript or other language resource collected by the linguist. Importantly, Eira (2007, p. 84) says that linguists must now act as agents for giving that authority back to communities and acknowledging their rightful authority as keepers of their traditional knowledge. They[8] say that to do otherwise means that linguists have not 'returned' anything.

---

8   I respect Kris Travers Eira's wish to be referred to by the pronoun 'they'.

When working within endangered language communities in colonised countries, Eira (2007, p. 82) says that outsider linguists operate from a position of unequal power relations between the groups. For example, Australian Indigenous people are the colonised people of this country, and they are still very much oppressed. Many live in third world conditions in the midst of a first world nation with horrendous outcomes for their mental and physical health and life expectancy and are in a state of ongoing crisis on many levels. Despite this, Indigenous people are beginning to assert their power as the authorities of their languages and cultural knowledge as perhaps one of the very few things that they assert any power over. This is weighed against the power of non-Indigenous linguists and other researchers, with greater levels of achievement in the national education system and the social and financial power that comes from the privilege of being a member of the academy, and that of being a member of the dominant group in the country.

Eira says that when linguists focus on the language, its grammar, structures and meanings, in isolation from the speakers of the language and the historical and current social implications of colonisation, they ignore the ground of language endangerment and can potentially unintentionally further endanger the very languages they are working to save (2007, p. 82):

> Because we still interact from a position of authority in the languages we are working with, we are maintaining the dominance of an outsider instead of acknowledging and supporting the authority of the community in their language.

2.5 Indigenous communities: Language maintenance and revival

For Indigenous people in Australia, as in many other countries around the world, languages and cultural knowledges have been brutally decimated by the impacts of colonisation. In Australia, of the more than 250 Indigenous languages (including more than 800 dialects), only 12 traditional languages are reported as being strong in the National Indigenous Languages Report (DITRC et al., 2020, p. 43). The report states that the languages that are considered relatively strong 'require purposeful and ongoing maintenance actions, so they do not become critically endangered'. The report also states that 'today, there is still a diversity of Indigenous language varieties, but the nature of that diversity has changed'; and it finds that there are around 31 Indigenous languages being reawakened by communities across Australia (DITRC et al., 2020, p. 58).

Hinton says that of the Indigenous communities that she works with in America, maintaining, learning and teaching their languages is inherently intertwined with a desire to maintain or regain their autonomy and self-determination, along with their identity, spirituality and cultural knowledge in a counter movement against the forces of colonisation (2010, p. 37). The same can be said of Indigenous communities in Australia.

In the context of language revival, Eira (2007, p. 84) says that sometimes the specialist knowledge and skills of a linguist are much smaller than what communities want from their language and it is becoming obvious that this applies to language maintenance situations also. Eira says that many Indigenous people say that formal linguistic treatment of a language is irrelevant or a low priority to the oral traditions of a living language. Further, the formal linguistic treatment of Indigenous languages serves to make the resources produced in documentation projects inaccessible (Hill & McConvell, 2010, p. 421). Hill and McConvell say:

> Products of documentation sometimes languish in archives unbeknownst to community members, or unfamiliarity with archive procedures can make applications for access difficult. Alternatively, documentation material may be physically available but inaccessible due to the format in which it is written up. Long stretches of interlinearised transcriptions or untranscribed material are of limited use in a moribund language situation and can be difficult to readily transform into user-friendly resources.

Hill and McConvell go on to say that despite the inaccessibility of material produced in 'pure' language documentation projects, it is vital that Indigenous people and organisations be aware of the importance of collaborative documentation projects that aim to train local Indigenous people to undertake their own documentation into the future. While this is a welcome and much needed development, many of the outputs of current language documentation projects remain locked-up in technical linguistic terminology, for example, in terms such as 'ergative' and 'transitive' that are unfamiliar to anyone but linguists.

Indigenous communities can lose control of their language and cultural information through university-based research projects or funding agencies. I use my own community's experience as an example of how a community typically inadvertently loses control of language and cultural knowledge through a language documentation project undertaken as a PhD program. In the 1970s and 1980s, a PhD documentation project was undertaken on Ngiyampaa. The outputs and products of that project—by way of the default copyright laws—belong to the linguist, who sadly has since passed away. Our community now has to negotiate with the linguist's children in order to have access to our language and cultural materials deposited at the Australian Institute of Aboriginal and Torres Strait Islander Studies (AIATSIS). Fortunately for our community, these people are very supportive, but the fact remains that we do not have control of that material. The same situation still exists today to a large degree, through research projects that are funded by government and non-government organisations. While there is now much more onus on the researcher to negotiate the research agenda and outcomes with the Indigenous community as outlined in the Code of Ethics for Aboriginal and Torres Strait Islander Research (AIATSIS, 2020a), which is a very positive development in itself, it is not usually the case that the copyright in the research outputs will be assigned to the community. While intellectual property rights are almost always acknowledged nowadays, they provide very little protection to Indigenous people's language and cultural knowledge. This point will be discussed in more detail in Chapter 4.

Some linguists believe that researching Indigenous people's language and cultural knowledge is harmless and unlikely to cause any lasting negative impacts. Musgrave and Thieberger say that linguistic research has a limited impact when compared to mining, and that linguists are simply asking people to sit down and talk with them or take them to significant places and they argue that this causes no harm (2007, p. 50). The harm is not immediate nor obvious to many non-Indigenous linguists who are used to the status quo and who might think that the loss of control of language and cultural knowledge as outlined in my communities' case is not significant harm. In fact, the opposite is true: the harm is hugely significant and can be ongoing for many years or decades after the research project has been completed and, often, long after the researcher themselves has passed away. This does not in any way take away from the obvious value of linguistic documentation when done ethically, but speaks to the need to ensure that Indigenous communities and individuals retain the copyright in their language and cultural knowledges through legally binding agreements.

Indigenous communities in Canada argue that a language is not saved by being documented; it is saved when a language is being used and transmitted orally (Hinton, 2010, p. 37). Richard Grounds points out that community members say that they would rather have the language on their tongues than in a dictionary. Grounds says that in small Indigenous communities, the needs of the community and the needs of linguists constitute separate agendas, while on the surface they might seem to be natural partners. He says documentation projects in small communities with very few native language speakers create competition for the very limited time of elderly speakers, which creates conflict (Grounds, 2007, p. 28):

> This conflict is a critical issue because the stakes are so high. The bearers of the knowledge that scholars are interested in are also the sole remaining people who can pass forward the gift of language on a breath-to-breath basis to younger learners.

The KLRC says that communities in their area were concerned that, despite all of the documentation that had been done for languages in their area, children were not learning the languages. As a response to the community's concerns, the organisation shifted its focus to support oral language transmission strategies (2010, p. 136). In a refreshingly honest case study that reflects on the impacts of ethnomusicological research in the Kimberley town of Derby and the Indigenous communities along the Gibb River Road (Treloyn & Charles, 2014, p. 177), Rona Googninda Charles articulates a situation that she faced in her own community when, after many years of research had been done on the junba songs of the region, the old people referred to the written records (the thesis) rather than passing on the songs as had always been done, orally. She said:

> Rona: Yes! I remember, I call him abi [brother], [he said] 'I'll tell you blokes. I'll tell you the story.' He was one of the main people responsible for teaching my sons. When they made a mistake, he used [to correct them]—[but] he said [to them], 'It's in the book, read it'.

This situation illustrates the underlying concerns of the KLRC and Grounds above, that is, the removal of knowledge from the Indigenous community and its cultural context. In the above case, the non-Indigenous researcher working within the community 'was granted clear privilege over potential learners in the cultural heritage community such as Rona' (Treloyn & Charles, 2014, p. 178). The authors put it this way (p. 179):

> Sally (and perhaps the reader) is confronted by a sobering example of not only discomfort but the symbolic violence of colonial Western discourse in action, wherein 'knowledge about Indigenous peoples ... [is] collected, classified and then represented in various ways back to the West, and then, through the eyes of the West, back to those who have been colonized'. Even the returns of research to communities delineate a 'discomfort zone'.

The Torres Strait Islander educationist Martin Nakata says that knowledge generated about the language in isolation from the history of the speakers is flawed, as it separates the act of speaking from that which is being spoken (Nakata, 2007).

This separation of languages from the traditional social context is of great concern to the KLRC (2010, p. 140) also, and they maintain that this encourages the younger generation to think of language as belonging only to the Elders or in books and not a part of their everyday life. This concern is core to the KLRC's change in its strategic plan to move towards a model of language continuation and maintenance strategies with a strong focus on oral transmission (2010). For the Miriwoong people, maintaining their language in the context of its relationship to land and their people's identity was the major factor in restricting outside access to their language. They say that their language cannot be viewed outside of the Miriwoong cultural context (Newry & Palmer, 2003, p. 104). For the Indigenous community or individual, their language represents their cultural heritage, connection to country and forms their identity.

2.6 Participating in the project of decolonisation

> As linguists, we are trained to act as authorities in language work. In addition, our positions in the social schema train us to maintain unequal relationships with language communities. Historically, we have moved through roles of benefactor, advocate, and empowerer. But all of these roles are based on a position of power—and ultimately it is power differentials which endanger languages. In my view, the next vital step is to understand our roles as participants in the project of decolonisation.
>
> Eira (2007, p. 82)

Linguists may have lost sight of the role that they can play in perpetuating language endangerment in their urgency to genuinely address language endangerment (Eira, 2007, p. 82). Eira's discussion of the issues is unusually honest and practical and attempts to address the core concerns. They point to linguistic training with its focus on the analytical processes of the language itself and say that it is this practice that perpetuates the status quo of unequal power relationships between linguists and the communities they work in and ignores the authority of the community in their language. Eira says that linguists now need to take a step back in relation to the ways they have traditionally engaged in language work and let go of control over procedures and analysis. I would take this to mean letting go of exclusive ownership of linguistic analysis, providing access to the tools of linguistic analysis, and recognising that the language belongs to the speakers and that it is their decision as to what to make of any linguistic analysis. It is in this way that non-Indigenous linguists can begin to contribute to the larger project of decolonisation. While Eira's own work was in the context of language revitalisation and therefore predominantly involved working with Indigenous communities as second language learners and with archival records, much of what they discuss can also be applied more broadly to language maintenance situations.

The impacts of colonisation are in no way a thing of the past and self-determination and reclaiming sovereignty for Indigenous people is a high priority. Eira says that this is especially true in the context of language revitalisation, and I would add here, language maintenance, both of which are high on the agenda of the larger decolonisation project (2007, p. 83). Eira stresses that linguists must get on board with this agenda if they are genuinely hoping to contribute:

> If language revival is ultimately reclaiming authority, reclaiming the right to be listened to, reclaiming respect for one's knowledge and abilities, and reclaiming power over your own business, then a linguist hoping to contribute will have to become part of that agenda.

It's worth repeating here that Eira asserts that the task for linguists is to act as a channel to ensure that stolen knowledge and authority flow back to communities. Eira goes on to say that if non-Indigenous linguists continue to maintain the role of the authorities and keepers of Indigenous people's knowledge, then they have not 'returned' anything, and they liken this to the project of repatriation of human remains and artefacts from museums and universities to their rightful communities.

Another important way that the non-Indigenous researcher can participate in the project of decolonisation is to share knowledge (Smith, 1999, p. 16). Smith says that academics must share much more than surface information, which she terms as 'pamphlet knowledge'. Instead, they must:

> share the theories and analysis which inform the way knowledge and information are constructed and represented ... to assume in advance that [Indigenous] people will not be interested in, or will not understand, the deeper issues is arrogant. The challenge is always to demystify and decolonise.

In order to re-engage with Indigenous communities who are pushing back against linguistic research in Australia, Musgrave and Thieberger (2007, p. 50, 53) say:

> We would hope that negotiation could lead to a mutually beneficial research relationship including training of local researchers to do their own recording so that there will be good records available for future generations.

And:

> We suggest that activities which transfer skills and capacity to community members have an important symbolic effect which can improve the engagement of the community in the research process.

This could be perceived to be a positive symbolic shift in collaborative linguistic research in Australia. However, this contrasts with the Centre of Excellence for the Dynamics of Language's guidelines for Indigenous linguistic and cultural heritage ethics,[9] which suggest training Indigenous people in the research community in roles such as office administrators or providing training in computing skills or interpreting skills, in line with the need for research to be collaborative where possible (Thieberger & Jones, 2017, p. 15). These guidelines were last updated in 2021.

It is difficult to know what to make of this kind of discrepancy, with the recommendations having gone from training Indigenous people to do their own recording in 2007, to office work or interpreters in 2021. It could be seen as an ever-changing strategy to somehow satisfy the need

---

9   legacy.dynamicsoflanguage.edu.au/index.php

for research to be considered minimally collaborative by major funding organisations, rather than a considered and meaningful approach to passing on important theories, knowledge and research skills.

However, much more is needed than symbolism and rhetoric and Charity Hudley et al. assert that it is no longer sufficient for linguistics to simply meet minimal ethical standards but that research must be inclusive (2019, p. 25):

> It is insufficient for research in linguistics to address current theoretical questions within the discipline or to meet minimal ethical standards set by institutional review boards; instead, in an equitable linguistics, all scholarship must be premised on inclusive research questions and epistemological and methodological ways of answering those questions.

In the New Zealand context, Smith says that there has been an important shift in the way that non-Indigenous researchers and academics have positioned themselves in relation to their work with Indigenous communities (1999, p. 17). She says that there is a positive move towards bicultural research, partnership research and multi-discipline research. Smith points out that it is important for non-Indigenous researchers generally to clarify their research aims and to strive for effective and ethical research when working with Indigenous communities.

In an example from ethnomusicology in Australia, Treloyn and Charles (2014) talk about the ethical struggles of a research site in the Kimberley. They talk frankly about how outside researchers and the Indigenous community have managed to overcome many issues that could have had the effect of freezing the collaboration. Instead, they have found that in honestly and transparently addressing the issues with the community and allowing themselves to be in that often-uncomfortable space, they have moved to a more equitable and bicultural model of research. Also, some years before, in perhaps the first well-known case of this kind in Australia, David Wilkins (1992) discusses his own collaborative research context. Also see Little et al. (2015) and Yamada (2007) among many others.

Linguists in Australia have long identified training of Indigenous people as researchers or co-researchers in linguistics as an important and necessary next step (Hale, 1972; Hill & McConvell, 2010; Yamada, 2007). Why, then, do we still have so few Indigenous people trained in linguistics in Australia after all these years? Charity Hudley et al. talk about the narrow focus of linguistics as a discipline, which excludes studies that would critically deal with relevant issues of race that directly affect Indigenous people within the discipline (2019, p. 26). They say:

> Ideological divisions that play out along differentially racialized cross-disciplinary and subdisciplinary lines therefore stifle deep discussion and research around race and racism within linguistics while also systemically marginalizing linguists from racialized groups to the detriment of the discipline and the profession. Such exclusionary boundaries must be eliminated, and community issues must be recognized as intellectual issues within a larger social justice framework.

Therefore, they say that it is distressing but not surprising that people of colour have not gravitated towards linguistics. When Indigenous people feel excluded or marginalised and not culturally safe, they find it very hard to engage or stay engaged in linguistics. This has certainly been my experience and struggle over many years.

2.7 Specialist training

The movement towards Indigenous people being formally trained as independent documenters and educators in and of their own languages has been seen in North America, with many Indigenous people undertaking doctoral programs in linguistics and the development of community and university training programs and manuals to train Indigenous people to undertake their own language projects and documentation (Hinton, 2010, p. 38).

In Australia there have been degrees and diplomas in linguistics offered to Indigenous educators since the early 1970s by the School of Australian Linguistics (SAL) (Black & Breen, 2001). The programs offered by SAL were, for various reasons, later merged into the Batchelor Institute for Indigenous Tertiary Education (BIITE). More recently, BIITE has offered a diploma of Indigenous language work, an associate degree of Indigenous languages and linguistics, and a bachelor of Indigenous languages and linguistics.[10] BIITE says on their website:

---

10   www.batchelor.edu.au/languages-and-linguistics/

> Batchelor Institute provides a culturally safe learning environment for Aboriginal and Torres Strait Islander people from all Australian states and territories.

The University of Sydney offers a Master of Indigenous Languages Education developed specifically for Indigenous people wanting to improve their knowledge of Australian languages and improve Indigenous people's employment prospects in schools and community settings:[11]

> The program delivers a broad knowledge of the linguistic features of Indigenous Australian languages as well as covering theories of language acquisition and learning. It integrates and applies the areas of linguistics, language education theory and practice to Indigenous Australian languages.

More recent approaches to providing training outside of the university context for Indigenous people in linguistics and language work include the TAFE sector, which was reviewed for each state and territory by Mary-Ann Gale (2011). Unfortunately, the program at Pundulmurra College in Port Hedland, Western Australia, no longer exists. Training is also offered by the not-for profit organisation RNLD, now known as Living Languages, which says in its mission statement:[12]

> RNLD's mission is to advance the sustainability of Indigenous languages and to increase the participation of Indigenous peoples in all aspects of language documentation and revitalisation through training, resource sharing, networking, and advocacy.

One of Living Languages' core activities is to provide training to Indigenous people around Australia. Their Documenting and Revitalising Indigenous Languages Program (DRIL) is aimed at giving Indigenous people the skills they need to develop, manage and operate their own language programs and projects independently to support the long-term maintenance of Australian Aboriginal languages. Other important aspects of the Living Languages training program are the Leadership Professional Development workshops. The goals of these workshops are to:

> Increase the professional capacity of Indigenous people engaged in language work, strengthen the participants' knowledge of linguistics, language documentation, and language revitalisation methods; develop the capacity of Indigenous language activists

---

11 www.sydney.edu.au/courses/courses/pc/master-of-indigenous-languages-education.html
12 www.rnld.org/

> to become trainers and share skills with other people in families, communities, and workplaces, and help to build a professional network amongst Indigenous language activists.

The trend for Indigenous people to gain specialised education to become language educators and expert consultants for their own and other communities could see the development of specialist training programs for Indigenous people to gain the skills in language work, documentation and leadership as the most important contribution of the academy to Indigenous language work (Hinton, 2010, p. 39).

Hinton points out that very few documentary and theoretical linguists are trained in language teaching theory or methodology. Importantly, she says that linguists planning to work with communities involved in language revitalisation (and, I would add, language maintenance and reclamation given the current trends in Australia) would be advised to receive such training, with the focus being on teaching endangered languages as opposed to world languages.

Creating new language speakers is at the heart of the trend towards the focus on oral language literacy in both maintenance and revitalisation programs. Hinton points out that methodology in language acquisition falls into the broad categories of classroom teaching of language, teaching of language through literacy, and language immersion and situational learning (2010, p. 38). Hinton also points out that the role of the non-Indigenous linguist in literacy programs is more clearly defined than that in oral literacy programs. She says that oral language programs involve intense immersion processes that sometimes entail, as a precondition, teaching of the language to the 'missing generation' of Indigenous people as second language learners in language revitalisation contexts.

Hinton points out that the language revitalisation situation is complex and often beyond the training of linguists, and that it requires a multi-disciplinary approach from the fields of linguistics, education and language teaching. She says (2010, p. 39):

> As the field of teaching endangered Indigenous languages progresses, training of both community members and their consultants must become more specialised to their specific needs.

Indigenous Native American scholar and language activist Richard Grounds says that the challenge is to work out strategies moving forward to align the endeavours of scholars with the needs of small Indigenous communities to ensure that living languages are being passed onto the next generations to keep the languages alive (Grounds, 2007). This is the responsibility of the field of linguistics and there is a need to develop and enact policies within the discipline that are in line with Indigenous community expectations.

Further and critically, Charity Hudley et al. (2019, p. 23) assert that the Linguistic Society of America's Statement on Race, while necessary, is not sufficient to combat racism, white supremacy and colonialism within linguistics:

> Scholars and students of linguistics are rarely trained to develop a critical perspective on how race and racism, as mechanisms of structural inequality, shape, and harm both our research and our discipline. This lack amounts to a 'race gap' in linguistics—that is, linguists have significant deficiencies compared to practitioners in other disciplines when it comes to the critical study of race and the inclusion of racially minoritized groups in our student and faculty ranks. There is thus a dire need for more research in linguistics—using tools from related social sciences as well as language-related fields and critical race studies, which are more welcoming to and structurally supportive of scholars of color and their work—to interrogate why such a 'race gap' exists and how to resolve it.

Likewise, the attempts of the Australian Linguistic Society (ALS) to address Indigenous people's rights within linguistics have been well intentioned but insufficient. This will be discussed in more detail in Section 2.8.

2.8 Guidelines, protocols and linguists' field guides

In 1984, the ALS, at its Annual General Meeting in Alice Springs, passed a number of motions that set out linguistic rights and guidelines for working with the Indigenous people of Australia and the Torres Straits, inspired by Jeannie Bell.[13] While these guidelines held out a great deal of hope for Indigenous people at the time, not much has changed in the practices of the field of linguistics in the academy in the following 35 years. This is in spite of the establishment of language centres across Australia and recognition of the importance of Indigenous languages

---

13 als.asn.au/AboutALS/Policies

by the federal government in funding these language centres and other language projects. The establishment of language centres came about following the release of *Keeping Language Strong: Report of the Pilot Study for the Kimberley Language Resource Centre* (Hudson & McConvell, 1984).

However, in recent years we have seen a positive shift in ethical linguistic practice that is driven by the demands of Indigenous communities themselves. Other places such as North America and New Zealand (Hinton, 2010; Smith, 1999, 2000) are well in advance of Australia in this regard, due in large part to the fact that there are so few Indigenous linguists in positions within the academy in Australia that might effect any real change. This is true for other colonised countries to varying degrees also, but perhaps it is because Australia is one of the few colonised countries without a treaty with its Indigenous peoples to date that the voices of Indigenous people can be all too easily ignored.

Some organisations in Australia are beginning to take a stronger stance on ethics in all areas of research that involves Indigenous people, with the continued development of guidelines and policies such as the AIATSIS Code of Ethics for Aboriginal and Torres Strait Islander Research[14] and the National Statement on Ethical Conduct in Human Research,[15] which universities use as the standard for their ethics boards.

Further, local Indigenous organisations such as the Innawangka Banyjima Nyiyarpali Group[16] and Wangka Maya Pilbara Aboriginal Language Centre[17] in Western Australia among others, have also developed their own ethical guidelines, protocols and agreements for working with Indigenous people in their communities.

However, this movement is still somewhat in its infancy in Australia, with the current AIATSIS code containing no compulsion for researchers to adhere to its guidelines. As mentioned above, universities adhere to the National Statement on Ethical Conduct in Human Research, which requires researchers to submit full ethics applications when working with Australian Indigenous people, and according to these, any research that involves Aboriginal or Torres Strait Islander peoples must adhere to the AIATSIS guidelines. Jacobsen (2018, p. 39) points out the AIATSIS

---

14   Code of Ethics | AIATSIS.
15   National Statement on Ethical Conduct in Human Research (2007) - Updated 2018 | NHMRC.
16   ibngroup.com.au/who-we-are/
17   www.wangkamaya.org.au/home

2. WHAT DO WE ALREADY KNOW?

guidelines encourage consultation and negotiation with the Indigenous community but she says that such criteria should be made mandatory. The ALS, in 1989, adopted a statement of ethics, which at item 4 states:

> Persons deemed to be conducting research not in accordance with the spirit of this ethical statement may be subject to disciplinary action by the Australian Linguistic Society, according to principles that may from time to time be determined by the Society.

The ALS does not state what form this disciplinary action might take and I have not heard of anyone being subject to discipline in this regard. Further, there are always concerns with organisations regulating themselves.

I would recommend that AIATSIS develop an online ethics-in-research course that includes, as a necessary outcome, the development of a research plan and the development of a legally binding agreement with the relevant Indigenous community. Such an agreement must clearly outline such things as copyright to ensure Indigenous control and ownership of language and cultural materials. The agreement should also clearly demonstrate that the research and the researcher meet the requirements of the AIATSIS guidelines. Indeed, some institutions are already outsourcing their Indigenous ethics applications to AIATSIS. Such a course could be utilised by universities as a part of their ethics processes for research projects that involve working with Indigenous communities.

Vetting ethics applications already takes place in some communities in Canada such as at Cape Breton University, which has the Mi'kmaq Ethics Watch (MEW).[18] In its research principles and protocols, MEW states:

> Any research, study, or inquiry into the collective Mi'kmaw knowledge, culture, arts, or spirituality which involves partnerships in research shall be reviewed by the Mi'kmaw Ethics Watch. (Partnerships shall include any of the following: researchers, members of a research team, research subjects, sources of information, users of completed research, clients, funders, or license holders.)

In the absence of similar controls in Australia, Indigenous communities and their languages and cultural knowledges remain vulnerable. Under the current model, the human rights of Indigenous communities involved in

---

18   www.cbu.ca/indigenous-affairs/mikmaw-ethics-watch/

linguistic research, or any other research in Australia, have been considered optional, with the researcher opting in or out as she or he chooses. The AIATSIS guidelines have been recently tightened with the requirement that all research with Aboriginal and Torres Strait Islander people go through full ethics clearance with the relevant university, as already noted. However, while it is recommended in the AIATSIS guidelines there is still no compulsion to ensure that researchers draw up research agreements with the Indigenous communities concerned—that is, there is still no real accountability.

Without some form of compulsion for researchers to adhere to guidelines and protocols, the loss of languages and all that is encompassed in those languages is at stake, as well as the possibility of any commercial gain that might assist in the struggle against ongoing poverty (Battiste, 2008, p. 508). Importantly, Battiste says that while communities are working this out for themselves and are often in a state of ongoing crisis at so many levels, the academy should not impose standards that contravene communities' desires to control their own knowledge:

> any research conducted among Indigenous peoples should be framed within the basic principles of collaborative participatory research, a research process that seeks as a final outcome the empowerment of these communities through their own knowledge.

Battiste stresses that in practical terms, this means Indigenous people must be involved in all stages and in all phases of research and planning (2008, p. 508). As Eira points out, previous models of the linguist being a benefactor, advocate and empowerer are no longer viable as each of these roles assumes the linguist is in a position of power (2007, p. 83) and says, 'I can only give a community something, if I have it and they lack it'.

Linguists who want to work on Australian Indigenous languages must get used to the idea that any research or work that takes place must be under community direction, jointly developing the research project and the research agreement in ways that ensure both that the community retains control of their language and cultural knowledge, and that the linguist will be able to satisfactorily address their research needs.

The majority of linguists' field guides, while generally well intentioned, do not offer any concrete strategies or sound advice around the important issue of protection for Indigenous people's language and cultural knowledge.

Exceptions are: *The Routledge Handbook of Language Revitalization* (Hinton et al., 2018), *Living Languages and New Approaches to Language Revitalisation Research* (Stebbins et al., 2017) and *Understanding Linguistic Fieldwork* (Meakins et al., 2018). These field guides represent the current positive trends in linguistic research and documentation (Jacobsen, 2018, p. 29) and are more in line with Indigenous people's expectations. For a review and discussion of fieldwork guides published between the years 2000 and 2018 see Britt Jacobsen's masters dissertation (Jacobsen, 2018). The review does not include *Understanding Linguistic Fieldwork* (Meakins et al., 2018).

Eira says that it is crucial to move from thinking about the issues to actually taking action in a different direction. They suggest that on a day-to-day basis, linguists can do some practical things when working with Indigenous people and communities (Eira, 2007, p. 87):

- Actively sit down and remember not to take charge (otherwise, we'll [linguists] do it in spite of ourselves).
- Listen most of the time; talk when asked to. People are so used to non-Indigenous people talking over them, they often need a lot of listening space before they are willing to talk.
- Avoid deciding things, even when asked to. Communities and linguists alike are used to the norm where the linguist or non-Indigenous person decides things. It can take a while to unlearn.
- When decisions are being made, avoid being the person 'holding the chalk' (Stebbins, 2001). The person writing up decisions necessarily has the role of deciding what to write.
- If someone asks an open question, leave it for someone else to answer. We [linguists] assume very easily that any question is directed to us.
- If someone wants a story, song, etc. written or translated, don't do it—help the person to do it themselves.
- Remember that the people we [linguists] are working with are the people with the right to know their language—not us [linguists].

The pathway forward could include both Eira's suggestions as to what to do on the ground, engaging with the literature from Indigenous linguists and scholars on the issues, some of which can be found in the references at the end of this book, and the importance of places where these issues can be openly discussed so that deep understandings and change can take place amongst other things. This will be discussed in more detail in Section 2.10.

2.9 Funding for linguistic research and language projects

2.9.1 Who gets funded for what and what are the real issues?

Major research funding agencies and universities have a very narrow view of what constitutes research and are out of step with the needs of Indigenous communities on the ground; language maintenance or revival programs are not considered 'research' activities and therefore do not attract research funding. Therefore, language documentation and language maintenance and revival projects are usually funded separately (Musgrave & Thieberger, 2007, p. 48). There are inequities between the funding for linguistic research and documentation and the funding for language maintenance and revitalisation and this situation can sometimes be a factor in tensions between Indigenous communities and non-Indigenous linguists.

In terms of Commonwealth funding for Indigenous Languages and the Arts (ILA), there is very little funding for language projects per se. While this funding program overall is worth $20 million Australia wide, $11.9 million is dedicated to operational costs for language and art centres, while the remainder is spilt between arts and language projects (Mahboob et al., 2017, p. 9). Mahboob et al. say that in 2015–2016, projects funded shared in $3.1 million and of those projects, only seven had a language component – between them receiving $383,000.00. The inequity in government funding for Indigenous language centres to undertake their own language projects and research is clear and Mahboob et al. (2017, pp. 11–12) say:

> If the value of grants programs is an indicator of Australian government priorities, languages are a low financial priority. The federal ILA Program is the largest source of government funding for Indigenous language projects in Australia, but even this program has distributed more funds to Indigenous arts projects than to language projects.

In July 2022, the Government announced that it would boost support for Indigenous languages and the arts with an additional $57 million over three years ($19 million per year).[19] The funding will be shared by 84 community-based language and arts activities under the Government's Indigenous Languages and Arts program (Office for the Arts, 2022).

This is a very welcome and much needed boost to funding for Indigenous languages but as always, we are not sure what will happen at the end of this three years and a possible change of government. The funding includes:

> Over $41 million shared between First Languages Australia and the network of 23 Indigenous languages centres located throughout the country.
>
> Over $6 million towards eight activities that bring stories to life and preserve culture.
>
> Over $4.8 million to support seven organisations to deliver targeted language teaching and learning activities.
>
> Over $4.5 million towards 44 Indigenous languages and arts activities, including cultural performances, establishing digital languages databases, and community workshops.

Major research funding organisations, such as the Australian Research Council (ARC), offer large grants for language documentation and other linguistic research. This funding is for the research project alone and does not include things such as administration costs (e.g., rent or insurances etc.) that are necessarily associated with running a language centre. In a major research project, these costs are usually absorbed by the associated university. Huge inequities exist between the funding available to Indigenous language centres or communities for 'language projects' and the funding for 'linguistic research and documentation'.

Musgrave and Thieberger say that large sums of money generally cannot be accessed by Indigenous communities whose languages are endangered, and, therefore, that the role of the linguist or researcher is crucial in accessing money (2007, p. 48). They go on to say:

---

19 www.arts.gov.au/news/funding-indigenous-languages-and-arts-projects

> This situation does appear to give grounds for the accusation that language documentation is often a 'colonialist' activity, at least when we consider models where control is located with external bodies and with researchers as their proxies.

It could indeed be said that language documentation is a colonial activity. It is no longer enough for non-Indigenous linguists to be concerned with the criteria they apply to their field within research funding frameworks and to worry about how they will minimally meet them. It is time now to positively and proactively engage with Indigenous communities' requirements to realise genuine collaboration and free, prior and informed consent. This will lead to better research outcomes for research for all involved. Pérez González (2021, p. 143) says:

> I suggest, from personal experience, that one's social conscience and the collection of linguistic data in minority languages should be inseparable actions in which teaching should be mutual and collaborative, not only with respect to collaborators but with respect to the community as a whole.

I agree with Pérez González's sentiments and believe that ultimately it is our own organisations, such as language centres, that are able to work in the best interests of communities and their languages and cultures. I recommend that organisations such as language centres be able to apply for funding for documentation and other linguistic research projects, engaging linguists, either non-Indigenous or Indigenous, to facilitate such projects. Many language centres and other Indigenous organisations have the capacity to undertake large funding grants; this is no longer true of universities alone.

Language centres have the interests of their communities at heart. They have the capacity to offer meaningful training of language workers in an ongoing manner through such projects, and to arrange language maintenance and revival activities around documentation and other linguistic research projects—for example, a master apprentice program or a language nest could be the site of a documentation or other linguistic research project.

Tying research to a language centre or other Indigenous organisation would be a simple solution to the perceived problems of having to make sure or prove that the research project is not only collaborative, but also ensures that the community involved benefits from the outputs of such research, such as maintaining and strengthening languages. Language centres have capacity in all these areas that independent outside researchers often say they find very hard to balance in a research project, as they are only in the community for short and intermittent periods of time and have other responsibilities to their funding bodies or home institutions (Musgrave & Thieberger, 2007, p. 53).

2.9.2 The requirement of Indigenous community consultation and agreements

As stated above, it is now time for major funding bodies such as the ARC and others to consider making major grant funding available to language centres and other Indigenous organisations that have the capacity. In the meantime, we have to find ways of addressing these continually frustrating problems that are currently hampering the work from both sides.

The desire of some non-Indigenous linguists to maintain control over research within Indigenous communities and their languages is not going to be viable into the foreseeable future. Indigenous communities are insisting on having a greater say in how research takes place within their communities, and they are now insisting on research agreements that ensure this takes place in line with protocols in their areas. Major funding organisations are reflecting this in their guidelines for funding and the expectation is that, at a minimum, applicants show that they have support from the community in which the research will take place. Musgrave and Thieberger (2007) have explored some of these issues from the perspective of non-Indigenous linguists.

Where Indigenous communities or language groups or individuals have no representative organisation, they remain vulnerable to research that does not protect their language and cultural knowledges. The onus then rests with the non-Indigenous linguist or researcher to make sure that they are honouring that community's basic human rights. They must take it upon themselves to ensure that in whatever research takes place, the language and cultural knowledge remains the property of that community or individual, through assignment of copyright in the research outcomes and not just the intellectual property, through the drawing up of a research agreement. It is a small thing to expect that non-Indigenous linguists and other researchers would undertake to respect and protect the human rights of Indigenous people.

Meriam/Wuthathi lawyer and businesswoman Terri Janke has recently published *True Tracks: Respecting Indigenous Knowledge and Culture* (2021). This book is a comprehensive and impressive guide to Indigenous Cultural and Intellectual Property (ICIP) across a broad range of fields, including visual art, performance art, languages and cultural practices. Terri Janke has for many years assisted Indigenous communities on these matters and has more recently been involved in helping Indigenous communities draw up agreements that would protect language and cultural information within research, either with universities or other organisations.

While this is a very positive and much needed development, there is presently no recognition of, or funding available for, adequate consultation or free, prior and informed consent or the drawing up of agreements with Indigenous communities in the research context. A development such as this would address the concerns of both Indigenous communities and non-Indigenous linguists and other researchers if done sensitively.

The initial idea and planning to undertake a research project happens well in advance of an application for funding a project or the taking up of a masters or PhD program. Negotiation with Indigenous communities should take place when the first seeds of an idea for a research project with that community are sown, not after the intended research has been funded or approved. Presently, this may mean that the linguist or researcher will have to go out of their way to plan and get free, prior and informed consent and agreements for the research project with the community in whatever way they can. Importantly, if consultation is done well, the community will have the opportunity to either accept, propose changes or reject the proposed research project. Indigenous educator and program director of Indigenous studies and Aboriginal education at the University of Sydney Lynette Riley gives some very practical and helpful suggestions about the process of working through free, prior and informed consent with Indigenous communities (2021, pp. 21–23).

This is the approach I took with my own PhD and consent seeking has happened and continues to happen via phone calls, Facebook pages and zoom meetings. At the time, I lived in Port Hedland in Western Australia and my community is scattered all over the eastern states and much further afield. While I was able to visit communities and do direct consultation on the ground in the earlier stages of my PhD, during the current COVID-19 pandemic I have had to resort to online meetings. This online way of communicating now commonly takes the place of meeting face to face in many sections of society and presents solutions in this space. Importantly, this approach can ensure that the research project has the best possible chance of being productive and successful for both the community and the researcher because consultation has taken place and can continue to take place. While this is far from ideal, it is the approach I had to take because there were no financial or time provisions in my PhD program to undertake more meaningful face-to-face consultation.

The lack of the provisions of time and financial support to undertake comprehensive consultation with communities urgently needs to change. I recommend that funding bodies, such as the ARC and universities, acknowledge that free, prior and informed consent by way of a research agreement is critical to research involving Indigenous people. Further, this process needs to take place well in advance of the application for, or ethics approval for, a research project. I would recommend that another category of smaller seed funding grants for community consultation needs to be established in the case of funding bodies. These smaller grants could be made available either to Indigenous organisations or groups looking to have research done, or academic linguists and postgraduate researchers looking to seek permission to undertake research with an Indigenous community.

This kind of smaller funding could support two-way community consultation and the forming of robust agreements. Further, an extension of the overall timeframe for the same purposes should be established for completion of a research project in case of honours, masters or PhD students that propose to do research with Indigenous people.

2.10 Decolonising linguistics

> [T]he new relationship between linguists and indigenous communities is a highly positive change, in the sense that human rights, dignity and equality are being respected and enhanced. Linguists, whether native or not, will have a role in language documentation and language revitalization for a long time to come, but their relation to the community and to the linguistic data they collect is being constantly redefined. (Hinton, 2010, p. 41)

There are very limited opportunities for Indigenous linguists, language activists, language workers and non-Indigenous linguists to have professional discussions around areas of ongoing concern (Bell, 2010,

p. 92). Bell talks about an Indigenous languages conference she attended in 2007 where discussions took place in an unplanned manner, and these became heated because there had never been a forum prior to this for concerns to be aired, let alone for resolutions to be found. She says that while some non-Indigenous linguists became defensive when confronted with the frustrations and anger of Indigenous people at the conference, many chose to hang in and engage in discussions.

It is clear from the literature that there is a great deal of goodwill on the part of many non-Indigenous linguists to address and move towards resolution of the issues. It is clear that there is also a huge amount of frustration, resentment and mistrust among Indigenous communities and language activists due to many decades of being mistreated in the research context and to the ongoing trauma of the impacts of colonisation. There is no escaping the fact that in the Australian context, as in many other parts of the world, working with Indigenous people involves having to deal with the impacts of colonisation to the present day. Many non-Indigenous linguists often feel as though, despite their best efforts to assist in finding solutions, Indigenous people are constantly attacking them. This is in most part not personal but a result of the fact that there are currently no real and genuine opportunities for Indigenous people to have their voices heard around these issues and for the two groups to work together to address the issues on the ground.

Opportunities for non-threatening discussion between non-Indigenous linguists and Indigenous linguists, language workers and language activists have to be a high priority. Unless a person is studying linguistics with a particular concentration on ethics, which in my experience is not at all usual, one would not come across the many great publications, only some of which are referred to in Chapter 1, that non-Indigenous linguists themselves have written in their efforts to contribute to a constructive conversation of the issues.

Conferences really are the only place where we all get together and enjoy opportunities to have formal discussions; however, these must be on the agenda, with plenty of space and time for them to occur. This situation has presently been disrupted by the current COVID-19 pandemic and most of our conferences are online for the foreseeable future. When we do come together, there is always the potential for the situation to become heated. It must be understood that what can be perceived as a personal attack is usually not personal at all; what it is really about is the need to speak out, the need to be heard and, if we can all remain grounded in the knowledge that we are allies with many shared goals, then I feel we can find our way to the other side.

The very few Indigenous linguists in Australia are often placed in awkward positions balancing the concerns of their communities with the concerns of their non-Indigenous linguist colleagues. Jeannie Bell talks about her role as an Indigenous linguist being seen by non-Indigenous linguists as a bridge between the Indigenous community and the linguistic community—a common and sometimes uncomfortable role for Indigenous people in her position (2010, p. 93). I agree that it is a very uncomfortable position. Bell points out, and again I agree, that we can then be seen by the community to be standing too close to the 'academic' linguists. Bell says that some people within her own community refused to work with her because they believed she might take away the language and 'give it to the university'. Importantly, she talks about the personal strain of being an academic and the challenge of maintaining her moral and cultural responsibility both to herself and to her community, and she points out that she is committed to ensuring she maintains the standards that her community expects of her in her roles as a teacher and a researcher. Again, I agree; my first priority is to my community and to the broader Indigenous community.

Jaime Pérez González, Tseltal (Maya) linguist from Tenango, Ocosingo, Chiapas, Mexico, and PhD candidate at the University of Texas at Austin, discusses the issues of linguistic fieldwork methods from an Indigenous perspective and says (2021, p. 135): 'Those of us who do activist work do so not by choice, nor due to academic requirements, but to honor our language, our ancestors, and ultimately our own existence on the earth.'

This situation speaks to the delicate balance that Indigenous linguists must strike when studying or working in the academy. Often, when Indigenous linguists raise issues of ethics, we do so at great personal cost to ourselves, in no small part because the issues of ethics in linguistic research serves to retraumatise us. Further, our voices are often silenced or ignored. The issues raised here also speak to why linguistics is currently not a culturally safe discipline for Indigenous people to engage in and, possibly, why there are so few Indigenous linguists in Australia. Charity Hudley et al. (2019, p. 23, 24) say:

> Compared to many other fields, linguistics remains predominantly white, even twenty years after Rickford exposed this shameful fact as 'an academic limitation for our field as well as a socio-political embarrassment' (1997: 171). It may be more comfortable to convince ourselves that linguistics just isn't for everyone, but to do so is to abdicate our professional ethical responsibility to make the discipline an equitable and inclusive place for students and scholars of all backgrounds, and particularly for those whose communities provide a disproportionate amount of the data that advance linguistic knowledge.

The end result is that the literature from Indigenous linguists' perspectives in the Australian context is very scant; while some Indigenous scholars aim to address the issues of ethics in research more broadly, to date there are only a handful of Australian Indigenous linguists and activists who have contributed to the literature of ethical research in linguistics (Bell, 2010; Couzens et al., 2020; Fesl, 1993; Gaby & Woods, 2020; Janke, 2009, 2021; Riley, 2021) (this list is not meant to be exhaustive). Some Indigenous authors have co-authored with non-Indigenous linguists, myself included.

While I feel a real responsibility to do that bridging between the two groups, I believe that there is huge impetus here for the broader community of non-Indigenous linguists. The challenge now is to actively engage with Indigenous people and communities on the ground, face to face and be proactive in providing real opportunities for discussion and resolution of the issues. Clearly there are some non-Indigenous linguists already doing this in small pockets around the country, but we now need to see a holistic approach from the field of linguistics more broadly. Charity Hudley et al. (2019, p. 24) say:

> Linguists—and especially white linguists, who bear the greatest responsibility for dismantling white supremacy in the discipline (Bucholtz forthcoming b)—can use our scholarly expertise and our institutional access to work for greater social and racial justice (Charity Hudley 2013). If linguists are to take seriously our responsibility to undo the racism and colonialism that were a founding motive of our discipline and that continue to do damage to our research, we must begin a process of critical, race-conscious self-examination and reparative and restorative work—for racialized language communities as well as linguists from racially minoritized groups, for practicing linguists as well as linguists-in-training.

3

The research project

3.1 Why did I want to do this research?

> As can be seen, there is much to do with respect to our ethical practices before we really have field methods in linguistics that are complete and inclusive, not only of the collaborator but of the community itself. I suggest, from personal experience, that one's social conscience and the collection of linguistic data in minority languages should be inseparable actions in which teaching should be mutual and collaborative, not only with respect to collaborators but with respect to the community as a whole.
>
> Pérez González (2021, p. 143)

My decision to undertake this research was primarily based on my own experiences of studying linguistics as an Indigenous person. Throughout my time both studying linguistics and working in the field, I observed the huge disparity between what Indigenous people strive for in our efforts to regain and maintain control over our languages and cultural knowledge, and the practice on the ground in the field of linguistics that has served to take away from Indigenous people the control of their languages and cultural knowledge and misrepresent or under-represent Indigenous peoples in academic publications.

3.2 How did I do it?

The research project was qualitative in nature and involved a small set of in-depth interviews with three Indigenous linguists and language activists and three non-Indigenous linguists. I formulated a detailed questionnaire that was used as the basis of generating discussion around the issues in an interview with each of the participants. The questions varied slightly for Indigenous participants and non-Indigenous participants but only so that the questions would be relevant to each group; otherwise, they were identical. All participants agreed to be identified in the research and their verbatim responses were sent to them for checking prior to writing up and publication. These interviews formed the basis of all of the primary data I collected.

The participants were selected on the basis that they had an awareness of and a deep desire to address the issues in a constructive and collaborative way. I did not seek alternative or antagonistic viewpoints, as the aim of this research is to focus on identifying the issues from both an Indigenous and non-Indigenous viewpoint and to endeavour to find common ground and a way to progress towards practical solutions, rather than gaining a broad range of views or opinions. Although, some alternative viewpoints do come out in the data and review of the literature.

I have chosen to avoid overly technical language as there are two specific audiences for this book: Indigenous linguists, language activists, language workers and interested Indigenous people more broadly; and non-Indigenous linguists. All participants agreed to being identified in this research.

As an Indigenous person undertaking research that includes Indigenous people, I have a responsibility to the broader community to not put myself forward as the expert but to allow the participants to claim their own statements and opinions. However, I have chosen to include my own opinions and voice in the research as an Indigenous linguist with experience both within the academy and in my own community and many of the communities in the Pilbara region of Western Australia.

I have chosen a semi-narrative approach to presenting the interviews; this sees Chapter 4 give privilege to the voices of the participants. It is necessary for me to be respectful to all participants and especially to the Indigenous participants and the broader Indigenous community in this regard. This is in line with the emerging Indigenous research methodologies that consider traditional knowledge and ways of being as a primary standpoint (Janke, 2009).

3.3 Who did I talk to?

I worked with three Indigenous linguists and language activists and three non-Indigenous linguists, who I will briefly introduce here. In the discussion that follows, I have divided the responses into two groups:

1. Indigenous participants: Jeannie Bell, Jaky Troy and Vicki Couzens = group A
2. Non-Indigenous participants: Margaret Florey, Kris Travers Eira and Felicity Meakins = group B.

Jeannie Bell is a Jagera and Dulingbara woman from south-east Queensland. She is a language custodian, long-time community linguist, language activist and educator who has lived and worked in Queensland, Victoria and the Northern Territory. Jeannie gained an MA in Linguistics from the University of Melbourne for her thesis, *A Sketch Grammar of the Badjala Language of Gari (Fraser Island)* (Bell, 2003), and has done work on reviving Badjala, a variety of the Gabi-Gabi language of south-eastern Queensland. Jeannie attended Monash University and, after graduating, she spent three years teaching linguistics at the Yipirinya school in Alice Springs, Northern Territory. She also trained Aboriginal interpreters for the Institute of Aboriginal Development. She was a senior lecturer in the Centre for Australian Languages and Linguistics at Batchelor Institute of Indigenous Tertiary Education.

Jakelin Troy is a Ngarigu woman from the Snowy Mountains of New South Wales and director of Aboriginal and Torres Strait Islander Research at the University of Sydney. She completed a doctorate in linguistics at The Australian National University on the development of pidgin in New South Wales (Troy, 1994). Jaky's research and academic interests focus on languages, particularly endangered Aboriginal and 'contact languages', language education, linguistics, anthropology and visual arts. Jaky has extensive experience developing curriculum for Australian schools, focusing on Australian language programs. She studied in Mexico and Japan, developing her interest in those countries' art, culture and languages. Jaky's current research is focused on documenting, describing and reviving Indigenous languages. More recently she has a focus on the Indigenous languages of Pakistan, including Saraiki of the Punjab and Torwali of Swat. Jaky is interested in the use of Indigenous research methodologies and community engaged research practices.

Vicki Couzens is a Gunditjmara woman from the Western Districts of Victoria. Vicki acknowledges her Ancestors and Elders who guide her work. Vicki completed her PhD in language and culture in 2017 at RMIT in Melbourne (Couzens, 2017). She has worked in Aboriginal community affairs for almost 40 years. Her contributions in the reclamation, regeneration and revitalisation of cultural knowledge and practice extend across the 'arts and creative cultural expression' spectrum including language revitalisation, ceremony, community arts, public art, visual and performing arts, and writing. She is Senior Knowledge Custodian for Possum Skin Cloak Story and Language Reclamation and Revival in her Keerray Woorroong Mother Tongue. Vicki is employed at RMIT as a Vice Chancellor's Indigenous Research Fellow, developing her project *'Watnanda koong meerreeng, tyama-ngan malayeetoo (Together body and country, we know long time)'*. Vicki is rebuilding the Gunditjmara grammar to facilitate a new phase of language learning through immersive experiences and home-based, family clan self-directed learning. She is currently writing plain-language resources for this community learning.

Margaret Florey is an Australian linguist whose work has focused on documenting minority Indigenous languages and training linguists and Indigenous community members in methods to reclaim and revitalise languages. Florey completed her PhD at the University of Hawaii at Manoa in 1990 (Florey, 1990). She co-founded the Resource Network for Linguistic Diversity, now known as Living Languages, in 2004. From 2009 until 2017, Margaret developed and managed RNLD's Documenting and Revitalising Indigenous Languages Training Program (DRIL) that delivers grassroots training across Australia to Aboriginal people in family groups, communities and Indigenous organisations.

Florey's training work has also taken her to international training institutes. She was a founding member of the InField/CoLang Advisory Circle,[1] and taught workshops at InField 2008 and 2010 and then at the Institute on Collaborative Language Research (also known as CoLang) in 2016. She also taught at the First Nations and Endangered Languages Program at UBC, Vancouver, in 2009, and at CILLDI (Canadian Indigenous Languages and Literacy Development Institute, Edmonton) in 2009 and 2010. Prior to her work with the RNLD, she taught linguistics in academic roles for 18 years, including at Monash University from 2000 to 2008.

---

1   CoLang is the Institute on Collaborative Language Research, formerly known as the Institute on Field Linguistics and Language Documentation or InField.

Kris Travers Eira completed a PhD in linguistics at the University of Melbourne on language standardisation and the Hmong in 2001 (Eira 2000). Kris worked with Aboriginal people reclaiming their languages for nearly 20 years, mostly with people of Yorke Peninsula, South Australia, and as the community linguist at the Victorian Aboriginal Corporation for Languages. They found that, in this work, it was clear that there were wide differences in approach between linguistics, professional practice and the priorities and pathways of people of Indigenous language communities. It was also clear that massive issues of post coloniality stood in the way, time and time again, of the perspectives and practices of the one group being understood by, useful to and embraced by the other group. Eira was responsible to and able to speak for only one side of this tension, so they spent considerable time in that 20 years theorising alternative positions for linguists that they hoped would enable linguists to work with what was happening in language revival communities, rather than the standard positions, which asserted predetermined views of what was and was not authentic language, and thereby maintained linguists as outsider authorities—out of touch with community business and offensively reproducing colonial power imbalances. They are not sure that they succeeded in this attempt—partly because it may be impossible to critique one's own discourses in public without being written off as holier than thou, not to mention unscientific, and partly because the grievous weight of post coloniality is bigger than any, or many, individuals, so that we are still not able to see its legacies clearly enough.

Felicity Meakins completed her PhD on Gurindji Kriol in 2008 at the University of Melbourne (Meakins, 2008). She has worked for 20 years in northern Australia as a community linguist as well as an academic, facilitating language revitalisation programs, consulting on native title claims, and conducting research into Indigenous languages. She became an Australian Research Council (ARC) Future Fellow in Linguistics at the University of Queensland and a chief investigator in the ARC Centre of Excellence for the Dynamics of Language. In these roles, she has led teams of students, postdocs and community members to document the languages of the Ngumpin-Yapa family, under the direction of First Nations communities, especially in close collaboration with First Nations organisations such as Karungkarni Arts. Meakins has also written over 50 papers on language endangerment and change in Australia, in particular the development of new Australian languages, such as Gurindji

Kriol. Underpinning all of these projects are a number of aims, including to honour First Nations languages and to recognise new ways of speaking by younger generations.

Amy Parncutt and **Jess Solla** are both non-Indigenous linguists and were interviewed with Margaret Florey as a part of the RNLD team. While I have not included all of their responses, I have included one or two that were critical to the discussions.

4
What did they say?

> I have this thing of why am I even bothering with the university system and academia, I don't need the Western system to validate my being, my knowledge, my anything; but they're all tools in the toolbox and there are opportunities through there to bring about change. We need to work with them until we have enough of our own Aboriginal linguists; we still need to work with the mainstream system.
>
> Vicki Couzens, Interview, 2016

4.1 Indigenous control of language and cultural knowledge

We are beginning to see a growing awareness among Indigenous people in Australia of the impacts that linguistic research has had, and continues to have, on Indigenous people. Currently, the majority of linguistic research has the effect of taking language and cultural knowledge out of the control of the Indigenous people to whom it belongs and perpetuating the image of us as subjects of research with no agency over how we are represented or what happens to our language and cultural knowledge. We can see that many non-Indigenous linguists are also becoming aware of these issues and are struggling in positive ways to work with Indigenous people to develop a more equitable linguistic research framework.

Yet despite this growing awareness among non-Indigenous linguists, and their best intentions, from an Indigenous perspective we are still a long way from achieving anything like genuine equity. This chapter aims to identify what are the barriers to realising genuine and equitable collaboration in linguistic research that meet the human rights needs of Indigenous peoples and the possible ways to achieve that goal.

4.1.1 Group A responses

In what is now referred to as a post-colonial environment (although some would argue, myself included, that Australia is not post-colonial), Indigenous people are coming from a standpoint steeped in deep trauma experienced through the loss of our languages, cultural knowledge, heritage and so much more throughout Australia, that persists through generations to this day. The growing awareness of the impacts that research has had on us as Indigenous people has left many, understandably, feeling a strong sense of protection over their languages and cultural knowledge.

Jeannie Bell, Jaky Troy and Vicki Couzens are passionate advocates for the rights of Indigenous people to regain control of their languages and cultural knowledge and see positive reform in the field of linguistics. All three women grew up in situations where Standard Australian English was the dominant language and they, like many other Indigenous Australians, were deprived of their traditional languages. Couzens says:

> Nobody can take my freedom of mind and they have no authority or control over my language; it's my birthright and myself and my family have the right to reclaim and reacquire my mother tongue. I don't care, the government or anyone.

We are seeing a growing and urgent need for Indigenous people to regain control over their languages and cultural knowledge. With the understanding that the academy or the field of linguistics offer no real solutions in this regard, Jeannie says that, increasingly, Indigenous people are beginning to realise that the only way to regain control of language and cultural knowledge is for Indigenous people to do the research themselves:

> They want the power to do it themselves and that's one of the things that Veronica Dobson[1] fights for all the time.

---

1   Arrernte Elder and co-author of Henderson and Dobson (1994).

Vicki Couzens feels that the Australian university system has failed to validate her custodianship of her language and cultural knowledge but says, importantly, that the same system can be used to effect positive change and build our own Indigenous knowledge base and evidence when we engage in the same system:

> it's a tool, we learn how those things work and we take those and turn them into tools to work for us. Therefore, I have a purpose when I'm going to do papers or publications to get that voice out there and talking about what we're doing and my PhD, because I see within the system that research is evidence which forms policy and resourcing, so we have to create our own because a lot of our evidence in our Indigenous stuff, we have to look overseas. We need our own evidence here as well, not that we don't have some, but we need to build that body of knowledge and evidence again.

This is a crucially important point; the more Indigenous people engage in the academy and publish on subjects that are important to them and their communities, the more we will see a push back against the ideas about us constructed by the Australian settler/invaders. For example, the Australia Indigenous historian Bruce Pascoe's book *Dark Emu: Black Seeds: Agriculture or Accident?* (2014), challenges the popular notion held by many academics that Indigenous people were, in pre-invasion times, hunter gatherers, by showing that Indigenous people not only farmed their land but also lived in villages with built houses, harvested grain crops and built complex aquaculture systems. In an article in *The Conversation*,[2] Tony Hughes-D'Aeth, a non-Indigenous professor of English literature at the University of Western Australia, says:

> Pascoe is an Indigenous historian and is clearly motivated by a desire to redress the serial denigration of Indigenous people. His cards are on the table, but this does not mean that he is not a rigorous and exacting judge of the historical record.

Couzens argues that all research and work within Indigenous communities must now be based on the foundational principles of a First Peoples First Framework, which requires following community protocols and including an Indigenous authority in all decision-making relating to the research or project:

---

2   theconversation.com/friday-essay-dark-emu-and-the-blindness-of-australian-agriculture-97444?fbclid=IwAR3RbeYnI_NBLuYUbcaytmpz9CSWPdGuvur_OucLYM0sZQHx3ym4J9yOglI

> In the day-to-day of working in those things you have to make sure that when we are talking about working in community with linguists and projects, etc., there has to be authority and control over that by ourselves, and linguists and all other people involved have to do their utmost to ensure that is the case.

This is the underlying ethos of the Victorian Aboriginal Corporation for Languages. Couzens gives an example of a community in Victoria that has been conducting their own language work without a non-Indigenous linguist for more than 20 years, she says this is their way of asserting their control over their language and cultural heritage:

> I'm thinking of the case study and Gunai Kurnai have been working for over 20 years with their Elders and they have not really worked with a linguist. They have done things their own way and maintain a really tight control over that. Sometimes language gets hidden within families or small clan groups where that knowledge is held secretly because that's how it had to be because you weren't allowed to have those things.

Another early example is the revival of palawa, a language of Tasmania.[3] The Tasmanian Aboriginal Centre (2021) says:

> The *palawa kani* Program was among the first in the country in which Aboriginal people ourselves learnt the necessary linguistic methods which have since enabled us to do all the retrieval work on our language.

These are poignant and powerful stories for everyone. The beginning of colonisation in this country saw many Indigenous people forbidden to speak language or being shamed and undermined for speaking their languages. In the case of Ngiyampaa, Tamsin Donaldson reports someone telling her (1985, p. 134):

> 'Dagos learn their own kids their own yabber' (or 'gibberish') 'so why are we shamed?'

This shame still persists amongst many of the older and younger generations. For Indigenous people to this day, the shame of 'not knowing' the language or cultural knowledge is very real and a part of the intergenerational trauma that Indigenous people in this situation live with daily. 'Gibberish', meaning nonsense language or the like, is a

---

3   tacinc.com.au/programs/palawa-kani/

term that was used, among others, to make people feel ashamed of their language, causing the abandonment of its use and advancing the take-up of English. This is another example of how Indigenous people's languages and cultural knowledges have been taken or stolen from them, this time outside of the research context. Importantly, this provides further impetus for Indigenous people to regain authority and control over their languages and cultural knowledges again.

Increasingly, Indigenous people are gaining the skills and linguistic knowledge to be able to work independently on their languages, but this is often a long-term endeavour, and, in many cases, there is an urgency to do this work. Necessarily, there continues to be a reliance on non-Indigenous linguists to help in this regard. Informal training and the passing on of linguistic skills to Indigenous people are emerging as important roles for non-Indigenous linguists, but Jeannie Bell says there seems to be some resistance or unwillingness to the idea:

> Some of them will tell them straight out, you know: 'Well we don't want you to do that, we'll do it ourselves and, if you are really helping us, you'll help us to it ourselves', but not a lot of people will do it.

The reasons for the perceived lack of support of non-Indigenous linguists in this regard could be many, including lack of training—linguists are often not trained in teaching methodologies and lack the skills to teach community members; time pressures—if a linguist is in the community for fieldwork relating to undertaking a PhD, they may not have the time to train community members and may fear that they might be doing themselves out of a job in the longer term. However, there is so much work that urgently needs to be done, in the foreseeable future, I cannot see this being the case.

Increasingly, training of Indigenous people to gain the skills to undertake their own linguistic research is beginning to be seen as an important next step for research funding organisations. Critically, Bell points out that Indigenous linguists and language workers better understand the needs of their communities and work with them in ways that make linguistics accessible. However, she says that often, when Indigenous people undertake to do their own linguistic and language work, they and their work are not valued by many non-Indigenous linguists:

> just trying to get some sort of understanding that, yes, we are linguists but we're not linguists like a lot of you are, but we still are doing linguistic work for our people, and we want them to understand how all this linguistic stuff can be useful for them, and not just heaping things on them that they can't understand and walk away and, 'Well that doesn't mean anything to me you know'.

I have had this experience myself and it is very disheartening when non-Indigenous linguists are unsupportive and, at times, even quite critical. In my experience, to have to constantly justify your intellect, your rationale and your right to take a meaningful place in linguistics is, in fact, demoralising and traumatising. Thankfully, there are also many non-Indigenous linguists who are struggling to deeply understand the issues and be as supportive as possible.

Core to Indigenous people's concepts around the control of language and cultural knowledge is how the systems of copyright and intellectual property rights impact on this control or lack of control in the research context. Jaky Troy talks about how she believes this should work in the field:

> I personally think that really ethical practice is that when you go as a researcher to do work with people, whatever you are doing research on, you're engaging with what they know and what they own and, by being the researcher and having the privilege of working with people and the privilege of writing up what you have learnt, does not ever give you any ownership over it; that's what I believe.

She goes on to say that at no point should a linguist undertaking research in an Indigenous community be able to lock away the rights of the Indigenous people that they have been working with and vest it in the researcher—in the form of copyright—or whichever institution or funding body with which they are affiliated with. She says:

> They should never divest the community of any of their rights around their information and vest it in these other people.

It is very often the case, unless otherwise negotiated, that the copyright in the outputs of linguistic research is vested in the linguist or the organisation that employs the linguist or the publisher. In some cases, this may be a language centre or other cultural organisation and this situation is also beginning to cause problems for Indigenous language communities whose copyright in their language materials sits with these organisations.

Troy asserts that Indigenous people are very often co-researchers and contribute significantly to the analysis of the language when working with a linguist in the field and, therefore, also have intellectual rights over that analysis:

> if the analysis is a jointly negotiated analysis, so for example if a language speaker is explaining how their language works to me, we immediately have a collaboration in which the language speaker has an equal partnership with me around the analysis. So, the language speaker has intellectual rights to whatever it is that he or she has put into that analysis.

The point that Jaky Troy makes here about intellectual property in the analysis of language is often overlooked by many non-Indigenous linguists and will be discussed in more detail in Section 4.2. I have mentioned it here because it is relevant to this discussion, as issues of control of language and cultural knowledge are intrinsically tied to issues of intellectual property rights and copyright laws and how these laws fail to protect Indigenous people's languages and cultural knowledge. This issue alone is one of the greatest challenges for us as Indigenous peoples.

4.1.2 Group B responses

> I think part of the 'how do you do it' is sharing the methods that linguists use to build that competence in the language; over and over and over again, really reinforcing linguistics isn't magic and it's not something we're born with, It's something we were taught, this set of skills, that's how we can do it and that's how we form hypotheses about a language structure and you know to really kind of work with people to see that process and to get them doing that.
>
> Margaret Florey, Interview, 2016

Non-Indigenous linguists are becoming aware of the issues being raised by Indigenous people and some have been actively involved in helping Indigenous people to gain the skills they need to be able to undertake their own language and linguistic work. Margaret Florey and Kris Travers Eira[4] are passionate long-term advocates for Indigenous people's rights to regain control of and undertake their own language work, and Felicity Meakins strives for best ethical practice in her own work with Indigenous communities.

---

4 C. Eira and Kris Travers Eira are the same person.

Kris Travers Eira's training and position have led them to develop a real sense of responsibility for ensuring that Indigenous people have access to the same tools and knowledge. Kris points out that languages are lost because of the imbalance of power between non-Indigenous linguists and the Indigenous people they work with. They say:

> if you are trying to help and you maintain the asymmetry of power, you are not helping. We are in this post-colonial environment, like it or not, that's where we are.

The ramifications of this imbalance of power, which is not widely recognised within linguistics, cannot be overstated. The linguist or other researcher is in a place of privilege, not only in terms of their education, resources and so on, but also they are often afforded a privileged position within the Indigenous community. This situation was clearly demonstrated in one research context in north Western Australia (Treloyn & Charles, 2014, p. 177):

> In the second instance, in this dialogue Rona sets out a clear rationale as to exactly how it is that Sally's collaboration with her elders could result in the removal of their knowledge from the community. In her experience, elders share their knowledge with younger family members when they feel they are approaching death 'They preparing themselves to die, when they want to give their knowledge.' By inserting Sally or other outsider researchers into this time-critical and relationally unique intergenerational knowledge transaction, such as in the gathering of data for inclusion in a thesis, the community runs the risk of losing that knowledge.

Likewise, Richard Grounds discusses the tensions that arose between the linguist and the community in a project to produce a dictionary within his own community and says that, in the end, the linguist won out, in part because the community did not have a representative organisation to adequately address the issue (Grounds, 2007):[5]

> In the colonial alchemy, putting the language into books is prestigious and turns the once-assaulted language into a highly valued commodity. I am not advocating squelching scholarly inquiry—I am, after all, a member of the academy—but at this very late stage in the life of the smaller language communities, we must figure out ways to ensure that scholarly endeavours benefit community language efforts, to keep spoken languages alive.

---

5   Documentation or Implementation | Cultural Survival.

Therefore, it is crucial that Indigenous people have and maintain authority over their own languages and cultural knowledge. Margaret Florey talks about the underlying ethos of the Resource Network for Linguistic Diversity (RNLD) training program Documenting and Revitalising Indigenous Languages (DRIL) and the practical steps they undertake to ensure that they are always working from the point of view that Indigenous people are the authority in their own languages:

> So really actively working on, as we've got newer trainers coming in, trying to sort of unpack what are the methods that we use and what are those foundational things that aren't necessarily about methods but are more about practice and our beliefs and how we enact them, and really making it clear that we don't hold any authority over this language, that we deeply respect the authority of the people there and that our job is to work with them to unpack their knowledge and to build their skills in their own language. I think that's very powerful you know, and people pick that up reasonably quickly from us and it's one of the things that builds trust very quickly in a two- or three-day workshop.

Florey's comments here about how powerful this process can be are very important because, as Jeannie Bell points out, some people still want the 'expert' to do these things for them because, in the main, this has been modelled by non-Indigenous linguists themselves for such a long time and it can take some time to unlearn. The process of giving Indigenous people the skills to do their own linguistic and language work is an empowering and important strategy and an incredibly effective mechanism for handing back control of languages to Indigenous people. Florey says that all linguists working in the field can participate:

> I think any linguist in the field can do that too, even if you're doing an apprenticeship by having people sit, younger people, sit with you when you're doing your language documentation or elicitation.

Felicity Meakins feels that this is a difficult space for non-Indigenous linguists to negotiate because the issues of authority and control are still complicated, even with a genuine desire to be helpful:

> I wonder whether some of what linguists can do is take more of a back seat. Most linguists are non-Indigenous and in trying to help, they might be interfering more than they realise. Taking back control over your intellectual property might not be helped sometimes by having a linguist at the helm. Linguists can be

> doing things making sure that when resources are produced, that copyright and intellectual property, stays with the community of course, but that still means a linguist is at the centre of a project and maybe that's not helping in terms of regaining control.

Meakins's point is valid, but linguists do not necessarily have to position themselves at the centre of a project, they can take a back seat and be a mentor and support Indigenous people to take the leading role and this can become a crucially important role for non-Indigenous linguists. Kris Travers Eira says that helping Indigenous people to undertake their own linguistic and language work can become an important motivation for non-Indigenous linguists:

> Back off and shut up, I do think we do a lot of perpetuating of that removal of authority and control. We have the agenda of making sure that other people know what we know, and I understand that it's a big internal mandate to pass on what you know—that, in itself, is an important motivation but where we step over the line is when we also think we know what should be done with that knowledge.

Eira places the passing on of linguistic knowledge to Indigenous people squarely on the agenda for non-Indigenous linguists. Critically, they identify the role that non-Indigenous linguists have long held as the people who get to decide what happens to Indigenous people's languages and knowledges and, correctly, they point out that this is where non-Indigenous linguists cross the line. This issue is dealt with in more depth in the following section.

4.2 Copyright, intellectual property rights and agreements

> At no point should somebody coming in and doing research with a community ever lock away to the researcher the rights or whatever institution they have come from or whatever funding body had provided funding; it should never divest the community of any of their rights around their information and vest it in these other people.
>
> Jaky Troy, Interview, 2016

Again, Special Rapporteur Erica Irene Daes (1993, pp. 8–9) concluded that, from an Indigenous peoples' point of view, there is no distinction between cultural and intellectual property, and global sciences' distinctions in this regard are artificial. The ownership and control of languages and cultural knowledges is vital to Indigenous peoples' spiritual and physical wellbeing in ways that are clearly difficult for the global non-Indigenous scientific community to comprehend. We could liken this to the divide between Christianity and science: if it cannot be proven through rigorous scientific investigation, it therefore cannot be real.

The issues around control of language and cultural knowledge are of direct relevance to the issues of copyright and intellectual property rights and, therefore, of critical importance to Indigenous people. With no effective laws in Australia that protect Indigenous people's intellectual and cultural knowledge, we are seeing a move towards the use of agreements that negotiate copyright in the products of research in a way that is beginning to address the needs of Indigenous communities in which linguists and other researchers work. The use of agreements that provide a licence to use certain materials in particular ways is beginning to be instigated by Indigenous people and their organisations. This is being done in order to address the huge disparity between Indigenous people's concepts of ownership and responsibility for language and cultural knowledge, and the global system of copyright and intellectual knowledge, which completely fails to address these issues adequately for Indigenous people. This situation also fails to address Indigenous people's human rights in their languages and cultural knowledge.

4.2.1 Group A responses

> The fundamental principles of never assign copyright, always have an agreement setting out the terms of your project. Our old people negotiated all the time between each other and mob so they understand about that process.
>
> Vicki Couzens, Interview, 2016

It is now very apparent that Indigenous people are becoming aware that the current copyright laws or intellectual property rights do not protect, in any meaningful way, Indigenous people's languages and cultural knowledge. While intellectual property is usually acknowledged in some way by the researcher or author, this gives no rights or protections to the Indigenous people's knowledge in the research context or publications. This sees

Indigenous people's languages and knowledge being used for all manner of purposes, usually without the consent of the language communities themselves. Just one example can be seen in the AustKin project.[6] This database has been built from information found in archives and published materials for many of the Indigenous languages of Australia:

> The AustKin database is a tool for researching Australian Aboriginal kinship derived from over 600 publicly available sources published between 1834 and 2014.

While the sources that the AustKin project have used are publicly available via archives and published materials, the original sources for those materials most likely would have been the outputs of research in Indigenous communities and published in the usual way, that is without the knowledge or consent of the Indigenous communities involved. The website then goes on to say:

> Please do not use words in the AustKin database to name your business, vehicle, racehorse, property or commercial product. It is standard practice to seek permission from the language owners through a regional language centre.

This seems quite paradoxical. It can only be assumed that no such permissions have been sought from language owners in the first instance to include their language and cultural information in the database. The materials used were in the public domain or in an archive, therefore available. I was certainly not consulted about the use of my language. Many Indigenous people may be very happy to have their kinship terms included in such a database but they must be given the choice to be included or not in the first place. I am not saying that this is not a very useful resource for people, including Indigenous people, but this clearly demonstrates the point: language and cultural knowledge can be used for seemingly endless purposes, once it has been recorded in some material way, without any recourse for the Indigenous people to whom the language and cultural knowledge belongs. In this case, as in countless other examples, Indigenous people and their knowledges are the subjects of scientific research. Jaky Troy likens the AustKin project to the entomological practice of pinning insects on a board for study and display (J. Troy personal communication, October 2019).

---

6   www.austkin.net

Troy says that from an Indigenous perspective, non-Indigenous linguists can only claim their own intellectual and creative input but cannot own the copyright in language and cultural materials. She likens this to the way copyright operates when buying artwork. She says:

> I think where the ownership comes in for an academic is in a particular paper, so, if you write a peer-reviewed article and it is published in a journal you should have the right to claim that piece of work, but the information in it, it's come from other people, you never own that information. Any more than these days when you buy an artwork, actually you don't buy the copyright, you can't just buy a painting and use it for any purpose you want to and so you've got a one-off use, and that's how I feel that is how all academic research should be viewed, and that's another reason why joint authorship should always be the practice. I don't see how anyone should feel that it's OK to get a whole lot of information from people and then claim it for themselves.

This is the underpinning of agreements that operate on a one-off licence to use language and cultural material. In a very positive development within the past decade, agreements that negotiate copyright are becoming more widely used by language centres and other cultural organisations. But the deeper issues are not widely understood by many Indigenous people or linguists; particularly around the secondary use of research materials as discussed above, and requirements of linguists in the academy to be publishing in an ongoing manner. In light of this, Jeannie Bell says that the issues of copyright and any proposed secondary use of language materials or data needs to be included in agreements and this needs to be sorted out in the very early stages of a project with plenty of time allowed for the discussions:

> I think it's got to be sorted out really early on, at the beginning, because otherwise a lot of the linguists in these universities are working as academics, not linguists, and, as you said before, it's that whole thing of publish or perish and I think that there's got to be a conversation about how that's going to happen in any particular sort of environment or any way that it's done, is definitely explained to people in a really clear way so that they understand. It's got to be really, really made sure over and over, that you do know what we are talking about. People are feeling that they are not being given enough information.

The point that Bell makes here is critical, as the ongoing publication of the outputs of research has been a major factor in Indigenous people losing control of their language and cultural knowledge in the research context. Linguists need to face this fact squarely and ensure that their research with Indigenous people meets the highest ethical standards, ensuring that research conducted with Indigenous communities and individuals does not remove their control over language and cultural knowledge. This is best achieved through robust research agreements.

Bell says that linguists often don't take the time to explain the issues of copyright in a way that is meaningful and ensures that Indigenous people understand the issues sufficiently with respect to what it means for them. She says:

> They make copyright seem so simple—'you just have to put that C and then put the ring around it' and that sort of stuff—but that's not enough for people to understand maybe sometimes. Why would anyone think that's going to stop you from not sharing the copyright in as much as we want you to? I don't know because it's one of those situations that's a little bit tricky, isn't it?

The current popular model for designing and using agreements is discussed by Claire Bowern. She talks about the secondary use of research materials and says that usually linguists expect and are expected to continue to draw on their research data for multiple projects. She discusses the secondary use of research data (Bowern, 2015, p. 154) and recommends that if the community is in agreement for the data to be used in an ongoing way, this needs to be built into the ethics proposal sufficiently broadly so that it will cover future similar work. Bowern goes on to say that many Indigenous communities will be happy to agree to this and will expect that the information they provide will continue to be used, as long as everyone is clear about what those uses are, and it is agreed upon. In a positive move, more recently some university ethics committees are not willing to approve ethics applications that mention 'future similar work', requiring instead that the applicant will need to go back to the relevant community to consult.

When linguists are negotiating agreements with Indigenous people, they must be very honest and upfront about what they mean by 'future similar work' or 'ongoing uses' and what this will mean for the Indigenous community and for the linguist. For example, once the language and cultural knowledge is made in a material form, that is, recordings and publications of any sort including theses, unless the Indigenous community have an agreement with the linguist that states clearly what this material can or cannot be used for, the linguist can then use it in any way they see fit and then others can use it also in whatever way they like. The linguist needs to give concrete examples of what this can mean for their knowledges; again, consider the AustKin project, which is freely available on the internet.

When linguists are encouraged to frame their ethics application and research agreements broadly enough to cover these secondary uses, so as to get around the problem of having to get further and ongoing permissions or negotiation with the Indigenous community in which they have undertaken their research, it continues to perpetuate and compound the problem that has seen Indigenous peoples losing control of their languages and cultural knowledges.

The move towards agreements can be seen as overly restrictive and troublesome for non-Indigenous linguists in the academic setting who are under a lot of pressure to publish continually to maintain their career and to continue to be able to apply for, and receive, research funding. The prospect of seeking ongoing permission for secondary use of research outputs might seem overwhelming to many linguists because it can be a time-consuming exercise, especially if people involved in the original research have passed away or moved away and there is no representative body such as a language centre.

However, if the community in which the original research took place never gets an opportunity to see or vet these proposed ongoing uses to which they have 'agreed' in the model suggested by Bowern above, how can they then have any say in, or control over, the ways in which their language and cultural knowledge is being distributed and used. And, do they get any say about how they are being represented by the linguist in these publications?

Most importantly, when the academic linguist publishes articles as a secondary use of data, often the linguist who authored the article loses copyright of that article to the publisher. This then twice removes the language and cultural information in such articles from the Indigenous community to whom it rightly belongs.

Using broadly framed agreements that loosely cover ongoing secondary uses of research data as a method to shortcut the process of gaining truly informed and ongoing consent is not only unethical, but also, critically, it presupposes that Indigenous people will not be interested or understand what might be being proposed. As Linda Smith says, the challenge for non-Indigenous researchers is to share knowledge about theories and analysis and about the ways in which information is constructed and presented (Smith, 1999, p. 16). Margaret Florey says that there are no excuses for non-Indigenous linguists to think that Indigenous people cannot understand linguistics:

> We say from the get-go, you can explain every linguistic concept in a way that people can understand and if you're not doing it it's because you're not choosing to.

This is critically important if we are to have genuinely collaborative research with Indigenous communities. Indigenous people being included in the research project in meaningful ways will not only foster great research outcomes but meaningful training of Indigenous people themselves as researchers for their own languages.

Teaching people how to use recorders alone does not constitute meaningful collaboration. However, Indigenous people operating the recording equipment in a research project would mean that that person who is operating the recording equipment holds copyright in those recordings and not the non-Indigenous researcher. This in itself would be a positive development and one that would need to be discussed in depth with the community.

The one who presses the button on the audio or video recorder holds the copyright to those recordings; this is a powerful truth. Indigenous people being the recorders of their own language and cultural knowledge in a research project could be a simple way to manage and keep copyright within the Indigenous community. However, would the non-Indigenous linguist or researcher who wants to maintain control over the research project want to give up the simple act of being the one to press the record button? If the non-Indigenous researcher was doing their consultation with the community in a genuinely ethical way, these matters would be explicitly discussed upfront. This is an example of what free, prior and informed consent looks like.

The current model of ethical practice and clearance in the university system falls way short of meeting the definition of 'free, prior informed and consent' from an Indigenous perspective and is seen as an exercise that serves the interests of the researcher. This model is already out of date and completely unacceptable to Indigenous people who have a deeper understanding of the impacts of research in Indigenous communities.

Importantly, Jeannie Bell says that when these agreements are being discussed, there should be multiple people from the community involved in the process to ensure that the community is in a strong position to contribute and negotiate the agreement and that they are able to articulate what it is they as a community truly want. She says:

> Perhaps it's got to be like a multiple number of people that have got to get involved if they are doing something, making story books or if they are doing other things. They might feel like they need to have more than one person say 'Yes, we have copyright of this, you don't. This is for our community, this is for our children, something that we are going to use over and over', perhaps because you are going to put it in schools or whatever.

Bell also says that agreements need to be flexible and able to be renegotiated at any point to make sure that all parties are happy, and everyone's needs are being met. Flexibility is important because linguistic research projects can often take many years. In that time community members might change their minds about aspects of the project or the linguist's needs may change. She says:

> you would need to be able to make changes along the way if that's necessary and say, 'Well what do you think, not be talking to this particular Elder?' Or, if it's with the non-Indigenous linguist, 'is that something that's going to work for you?'

She points out that ongoing renegotiation is really important at another level because people in communities are not in the university system, and may not always remember what was agreed to or the way things were done in the first instance:

> People have got to understand what it all means. Sometimes people will say 'Well you know, how we did it that other time, you know when we were doing that other book', and maybe people have forgotten how we did it last time and we need to go over it again and make sure.

In research projects that span many years, the linguist/s might visit the community perhaps once or twice a year. While the linguist is often working on the project full time back at their institution, the Indigenous people with whom they have been working resume their daily lives until the next field visit. It must not be assumed that people will remember the way something happened previously, and time must be taken to ensure that whatever the linguist is proposing is clearly and comprehensively understood. Bell uses the Australian historian Mary Anne Jebb as an example of a researcher who does this well and deeply understands the issues and enacts this in her own professional practice:

> She's always got people with her so that she's not doing it on her own; she's always really honest about what she's doing and just in terms of that particular person from that community wasn't happy with this or we had to move this over to here. She's really good at making sure that all the t's are crossed and all of that kind of stuff. She has been doing some good work hasn't she.

In community language centres around Australia, agreements around copyright and the licence to use language and cultural materials are now becoming more and more widely used. Several language centres in Western Australia employ these agreements both in-house for their work with language specialists and with outside researchers. When asked about these agreements in a research context, Jaky Troy says:

> these kinds of agreements can work because it is just good common sense and its good form. If you want to be fair with people, then you have to recognise what their contribution has been to your thinking and to whatever you write up from your thinking. Equally I think communities need to consider that in the event that none of your successors are around [at the time of your death] that that information isn't then just locked away forever because there is no one who's inherited the copyright.

Troy talks about the critical importance of succession planning in copyright of language and cultural materials. Linguists and others who might need to seek permission to use the same in the future will have a better chance of finding the right person to consult.

This is a concern for Indigenous linguists, activists and language workers and communities and non-Indigenous linguists alike. Couzens agrees and points out that the agreed-upon uses have to be spelled out specifically:

> There should be agreements that you can use my tape [recording] as a resource for this, this, and this and, when I die, the authority goes to my eldest daughter or whatever, we need those succession plans as well. You can will copyright; it survives 70 years after your death.

Non-Indigenous linguists are key to making sure that these kinds of agreements and succession planning for copyright take place in their own research contexts. Also, non-Indigenous linguists need to make decisions about what will happen to their materials when they die and have succession plans in place, ideally to repatriate the same materials back to the communities from which they originated. They also need to ensure that they have good descriptions about who provided what materials and where that material is or will be located.

Jaky Troy again says that joint authorship is critical in helping to protect Indigenous people's cultural knowledge in the academic setting, and journals now are more and more accepting of jointly authored papers where the roles of the co-authors are very different. An Indigenous linguist myself, I have recently published an article with a non-Indigenous linguist, Alice Gaby (Gaby & Woods, 2020). Troy says:

> The joint authorship one is absolutely critical, and also not necessarily to put yourself forward as the primary author or the researcher; if your teacher, or several teachers or the community have done more than you have, name it and don't claim first authorship; credit where it is due. Journals are actually now accepting this joint or multiple authorship.

4.2.2 Group B responses

> I think that it is so important for copyright and intellectual property to stay with the communities in two different ways. For primary documentation work—like dictionaries and plant and animal books—copyright and intellectual property need to be assigned to communities and I think the easiest way to do that is to publish with Indigenous presses. Many of our books have been published with Batchelor Press, and we just had a collection of narratives published by Aboriginal Studies Press. Those are presses you don't have to have arguments with you just say copyright stays with the community and it's totally straightforward and that's really good.
> Felicity Meakins, Interview, 2016

There are a range of responses from non-Indigenous linguists here. While Meakins sees no real barriers to negotiating some aspects of what copyright might rightfully stay with the community and ways this can be achieved, others feel that the issues are too complex or that there is a lack of understanding around copyright generally on both sides.

Felicity Meakins is among a growing cohort of young non-Indigenous linguists who see no real justifiable barriers to truly ethical linguistic practice; however, they need guidance and a framework to work within, especially within the academy, which Vicki Couzens calls 'the colonial brick wall'.

Kris Travers Eira says that Indigenous people's concept of intellectual property rights and copyright creates a confusion of the issues:

> I think this word copyright is taken by people to have much wider range in power than it actually does. Copyright is literally about the right to copy. I've noticed that people hope that it has much bigger implications about right to use in all sorts of ways, that copyright law just doesn't go anywhere near.

Eira picks up on the huge disparity between what copyright and intellectual property rights offer, or rather don't offer, Indigenous people and what Indigenous people actually want in terms of the right to control and manage their cultural materials. They say:

> the system of copyright and the system of how Aboriginal people are seeing their ICIP [Indigenous Cultural and Intellectual Property], that's been talked about a lot, but there is this massive disparity in mainstream law that doesn't anything like come to grips with that other system, so that's sort of a problem that sits there no matter what you do with it.

While Felicity Meakins says that publishing with Indigenous presses, in most cases, is an easy way to negotiate copyright in certain community-based productions such as dictionaries and text collections, it must be kept in mind that these small independent publishers are vulnerable to financial challenges, as is the case for all not-for-profit Aboriginal community-controlled organisations. Felicity Meakins says it gets trickier when it comes to academic outputs such as grammars, not just because the publishers find this hard to negotiate but because, in these types of cases, she says there are two levels of copyright:

> We ended up having all the sound files copyrighted to the community, but we couldn't copyright the book itself to the community, and I was in two minds about it because on the one hand, I think the actual language should have copyright and intellectual property attributed to the community and we were successful in that, but the analysis of the language in a grammar is actually coming from the linguist and not from the community.

> I think in that sense I can see that there's two kinds of copyright in grammars and other analytical work, and books should be able to have copyright over different parts of it in some ways.

As discussed above, Jaky Troy says this is a grey area in linguistics. She argues that the analysis of language is a joint exercise and that the Indigenous language teacher who works with linguists is more like a co-researcher in this regard—one who, in order to teach linguists about their language and how it works, also undertakes linguistic analysis. One of the practical ways around this is overtly recognising the speakers' ownership of the language and negotiating a licence to represent their language in books or other publications.

Kris Travers Eira says that the ICIP over the language data is not controversial in the legal sense, although it can be controversial for Indigenous people sometimes. They highlight the current default position:

> but what is said about it, is considered to belong to the researcher, so the copyright of the entire thing then would, by default, belong to the researcher and the bits within it, which are data from the Aboriginal person whose language it is, that's still their intellectual property, is kind of the default way of seeing it. The copyright isn't for the language and can't ever be for the language; languages are not legally copyrighted.

We can plainly see that the default position of the global research community is totally out of touch with Indigenous people's views on these matters. Critically, it is exactly at this point that Indigenous people lose control of their languages and cultural knowledges to the researcher.

Eira has seen cases in which linguists have assigned their copyright to the community they have been working with, but this is meaningless once an article or paper is published in an academic journal; if the copyright is not renegotiated, the publisher then owns it:

> their name can be on as author or co-author but the copyright belongs to the communities and that doesn't seem to be hugely problematic if you are in control of the publishing, but I think what a lot of people who aren't academics don't realise is that usually when you publish, you lose copyright, the publisher owns the copyright, so that's a different battle, it's a part of the whole thing about copyright doesn't mean what people think it means.

This point was raised by Jeannie Bell above and the situation is not very well known by Indigenous people who are not familiar with the university system and copyright and contract law. As previously mentioned, this has some serious implications for Indigenous people in terms of their ongoing concerns around the control and management of their language and cultural rights.

Importantly, Felicity Meakins points out that the ethics forms that she has seen don't mention copyright:

> Actually, our ethics forms don't say anything about copyright. I know the ethics forms we use here and the ones I know at Melbourne University, they don't say anything about copyright.

The ethics protocols laid down by the NHMRC, to which universities adhere, do not currently address the possibility that copyright in the research outputs must be negotiated with the Indigenous community in which the research takes place. The mantra in human ethics to 'do no harm' does not consider the tremendous harm that has already been done and continues to be perpetuated by the current model of ethical research. Britt Jacobsen says (2018, p. 38):

> The outdated ethics criteria of 'do no harm', which is common to many research guidelines, fails to hold researchers to account for doing more than satisfying their own academic interests.

However, the new AIATSIS code does address copyright in the research context. It states: 'It is also important to note that ICIP rights are not well reflected in Australian copyright law. While copyright laws cover things in material form, ICIP rights extend to all forms of tangible and intangible heritage and culture' (AIATSIS, 2020b p.8).

Encouragingly, some more recently published linguist's field guides go beyond the currently outdated ethical standards; however, Jacobesen says that many do not (2018, pp. 10–15). Jacobsen importantly highlights the fact that the national body for Indigenous research in Australia itself does not currently address these issues adequately:

> The Australian Institute of Aboriginal and Torres Strait Islander Studies (AIATSIS) Guidelines for Ethical Research in Australian Indigenous Studies (2012) encourages consultation and negotiation with the community, as well as community input

and control of the research process. While this is a step in the right direction, such criteria should be made mandatory, rather than simply encouraged, for a project to receive funding.

While the new AIATSIS code[7] acknowledges that intellectual property rights do not afford the same protection as copyright law, and while the institution has strengthened and expanded its code, it still does not make its code mandatory.

Margaret Florey says that the issue of copyright is a very intangible concept. Further, she says that we should be looking to co-authorship because authorship and copyright merge:

> I think that maybe rather than copyright, that authorship is the thing for us to be talking about you know, that really sort of overt recognition of who the authors are, in some ways copyright and authorship merges because if you are an assigned author then you also hold more rights over a publication. I think all of these things flow from each other; if people are trying to work from a more ethical basis and a more respectful basis then they will, by their nature, also negotiate authorship relationships.

Co-authorship provides an important and valid alternative strategy to deal with the issues of copyright in publications for individual authors, and this is already an acceptable way to publish in academic journals. However, it does not deal with the issue of community copyright. The co-authoring of a dissertation is something that isn't generally accepted within the arts and humanities, but Felicity Meakins says that it is worth looking to the field of science for ways that co-authorship can work in a research context:

> it's probably worth looking to science, so in science they have a slightly different kind of dissertation where students write a series of publishable papers and everybody who has contributed to those papers is an author on it, and that would include the major Indigenous contributors, so I think, within arts and humanities we don't have the structure set up to do that yet but I think we should be looking towards the sciences to try and make some inroads into that and to appropriately attribute authorship to Indigenous collaborators when they have been major contributors to research.

---

7   aiatsis.gov.au/sites/default/files/2020-10/aiatsis-code-ethics.pdf

This is especially important in the field of documentary linguistics where, as Jaky Troy points out, there could be a case for considering the analysis of language as a joint exercise in some cases, with the language teachers being considered co-researchers. There is at least one example of a master's thesis being co-authored with a Warlpiri community member, that of Simon Fisher at Charles Darwin University.[8]

Kris Travers Eira believes that agreements that negotiate copyright can work in the academic research context:

> I don't think that interferes with that problem of points and career and all of that, as far as I know it, it doesn't interfere with all of that.

A shift in this direction in the humanities and arts would certainly be beneficial for Indigenous people but it could be a long time coming. In the meantime, agreements that include a licence to use language and cultural materials and co-authoring are becoming an alternative way of negotiating copyright in the research context within Indigenous language centres and communities. Generally, there is an acceptance that this is becoming common practice in linguistics. Felicity Meakins says:

> I think it's an appropriate way of doing things, it's how things are; that knowledge is not the knowledge of the non-Indigenous academic. I know that KLRC now has extensive agreements that outline that kind of thing when you undertake work within their auspice. For example, in our work at Balgo, you enter into an agreement with the KLRC, I think that's really great.

However, the use of agreements between researchers and Indigenous communities is a relatively new arrangement and the practice is a cause of some concern for non-Indigenous linguists. Margaret Florey feels that she doesn't know enough about how these kinds of agreements might work from a legal perspective:

> I feel like I don't know enough about copyright and who might hold it, I guess, or the way that the licence works and I think for me the questions would be from a legal perspective how you actually would manage that and what steps somebody would legally be able to take if the licencing is breached. I think often those kinds of licences are negotiated without a deep understanding of the law

---

8   researchers.cdu.edu.au/en/studentTheses/pikilyi-water-rights-human-rights

and so you might find you've got no rights to do anything about it if the licence is breached. I hope it's what would come out of respectful relationships.

Florey's question about the effectiveness of agreements and licences if tested is valid. I think that, in time, Indigenous people will increasingly progress the development of these kinds of licences and agreements with legal advice from specialists in the area of intellectual property such as Indigenous lawyer Terri Janke[9] and others; this is already taking place within some Indigenous organisations. Terri's lived experience as a Wuthathi/Meriam person gives her deep insight into the issues.

Kris Travers Eira says that negotiating these kinds of agreements with universities might be problematic because of the way they view research from the lens of hard science, which can have commercial implications for the researcher. They say:

> It's just a matter of getting the contract right and sometimes universities can be a bit stubborn about this sort of stuff. That's partly because most of the research in universities is about hard science, which is a very different issue because there, you're talking about commercialisable [research products], it's a whole different ball game. We don't have that problem in our discipline but that's what the university concerns argue towards and that's why they can find it difficult to move out of that, because it has huge ramifications for hard sciences but almost no ramifications for social sciences—we are not making new plants and making a fortune on the food they produce.

The point that Eira makes here about the potential 'commercialisable' value of research in the hard sciences does have potential implications for Indigenous peoples in social science research contexts also, such as linguistics. I think that there is some overlap here between the sciences that is often overlooked. Marie Battiste says Indigenous people are becoming more aware of the potential to alleviate many of their economic and social problems through the commercialisation of their cultural knowledge in their own time and ways (2008, p. 503).

James Cook University, through the Tropical Indigenous Ethnobotany Centre, recognises the issues and seeks to help the Indigenous peoples of Queensland to 'record, document and research cultural plant use

---

9   www.terrijanke.com.au

knowledge, which could be of mutual benefit to Traditional Owners and their partners'.[10] Importantly, one of the functions of this program is protection of Indigenous intellectual and cultural property rights over plants. Bruce Pascoe talks about the potential commercial value to Indigenous people in native plant knowledges:[11]

> '[We're] trying to organise ourselves so large food companies don't put a brand on it and dispossess us once again… we don't want to be dispossessed twice.' Bruce emphasises that Indigenous people must be able to sell and take ownership of the native food industry and process.

Non-Indigenous linguists may not think of these issues when working with Indigenous people, and plant knowledge and use is often recorded, sometimes in conjunction with other researchers such as botanists. This is one area of cultural knowledge that has great potential to help Indigenous people alleviate poverty in our communities. While often this knowledge is given back to the communities, sometimes in the form of beautifully illustrated plant books, what then happens to the intellectual knowledge that has been collected by the researcher? Goodwill alone does not address the issues, and agreements are necessary.

There are some notable exceptions, particularly the work of Glenn Wightman (see Hector et al., 2012; Raymond et al., 2018) and Felicity Meakins (see Meakins et al., 2019; Meakins & McConvell, 2021; Wadrill et al., 2019; Wadrill et al., 2015). Both of these authors have made concerted efforts to explicitly acknowledge community ownership of language and cultural knowledge, and co-author with their co-researchers. They set a very good example of what can and should be achieved.

Margaret Florey and Felicity Meakins both say that there is often a lot of goodwill and there are good working relationships between Indigenous people, communities and non-Indigenous linguists, and that these ways of working together can be very productive. Meakins says, however, that some non-Indigenous linguists don't do this well and these agreements do offer some protections:

---

10   www.jcu.edu.au/australian-tropical-herbarium/research-and-programs/tropical-indigenous-ethnobotany-centre-tiec
11   greatersydneylandcare.org/in-conversation-with-bruce-pascoe/

> We didn't do that when I was working at Katherine Language Centre, and I think it was OK because the linguists that we worked with from the university generally had a lot of goodwill, but it didn't protect the language centre from linguists who might not have had a lot of goodwill. I think you do need to have formal agreements in place because there are people who do the wrong thing, and you need some way of protecting communities against those people.

Meakins raises an important point here: while we know that many non-Indigenous linguists work hard to build respectful collaborative working relationships with the Indigenous people and communities that they undertake their research with, just as many do not and have caused and continue to cause great harm both to the Indigenous people and communities that they work with and the field of linguistics generally.

Further, it would be wonderful to imagine that respectful relationships and collaborations would protect Indigenous people's language and cultural knowledge, but, as Jeannie Bell points out above, this is not always the case and Indigenous people often get taken advantage of by the non-Indigenous linguist who has had a long association with the community. In many of these cases, the non-Indigenous linguist is afforded a privileged place in the community and much trust and often love is placed in them, but this will not ensure that the non-Indigenous linguist will vest the copyright of their research or project with the Indigenous people they have been working with and to whom it rightly belongs. They have a position back in their institution and the pressure to publish from the research is unrelenting; this fact alone is one of the major causes of the loss of Indigenous people's language and culture.

The academy must acknowledge this dilemma and address it within their institutional ethics processes, ensuring that ethics applications for researchers working with Indigenous people have an agreement in place that negotiates the copyright in research outputs in a way that ensures protection of Indigenous people's languages and knowledges.

However, linguists wanting to do the right thing by Indigenous people do not have to wait for the academy to change its processes; they can change their own practices in this regard. Seeking permission for future uses of data, for example, is not a hard thing to do and you can design your consent form to take this into account as I have done; you will also want to include succession plans for the copyright of the data. I know that if any of the co-researchers involved in my PhD became unable to be contacted for any reason, I would have to go to appropriate family members to get that permission and this is standard practice in Indigenous communities. It can take a bit more time but planning for a new publication is often known well in advance of the publication date and if permissions are sought early on, there should not really be any or much delay. It is simply a matter of goodwill on behalf of the linguist, Indigenous or non-Indigenous. This is the highest possible standard of respectful and ethical collaboration; from an Indigenous point of view, it is the way business is done in the normal course of things and is expected.

This does not supplant the need for formal agreements or licences to use language and cultural materials, but it is one thing that linguists can do to show respect for the Indigenous people with whom they propose to undertake research. Most importantly, it demonstrates to ethics committees that this is becoming the practice in linguistics and the more it does become standard practice, over time the more acceptable it becomes to the academy.

4.3 Community directed research: Identifying communities' research needs

> We need to develop a whole new approach to what research is in the context of Australian languages. Our languages are dying, let's be honest, they go to sleep. I don't think this country can sustain a model where people come in and do research with our people into the future that isn't going to serve the purposes of the communities that research is being done with, so that should be the starting point.
>
> Jaky Troy, Interview, 2016

Linguistic documentation of Indigenous languages has provided Indigenous people with the linguistic resources to maintain and revitalise our languages. The process of revitalising a sleeping language involves a lot of hard work and commitment on behalf of Indigenous community members. This can take many years if not decades and usually requires the Indigenous people who have taken on this challenge to gain at least some understanding of linguistics. This is because the outcomes of documentation projects and other linguistic research that Indigenous communities might use are presented in pompous linguistic terminology that has the effect of locking the language away.

Indigenous people are now beginning to question the value to themselves of linguistic documentation, the outputs of which are generally 'given back' to the communities in the form of complex grammars and, in the majority of cases, overly complex dictionaries (as noted by Corris et al., 2004). These outputs have not been designed with Indigenous communities in mind, but other linguists. Decades of documentation have not helped Indigenous communities to keep their languages on their tongues or to make language maintenance or revival easy. Indigenous people are beginning to understand that documentation alone will not 'save' their languages, when saving a language from a non-Indigenous linguist's point of view is to 'document it before the last speakers die'. This position is becoming untenable when we are being told by non-Indigenous linguists themselves that our languages are severely endangered and in the next however-many years, our languages, and everything that they encompass, will all be gone.

Indigenous people are now pushing back and saying that the situation must change, that language documentation and other linguistic research must be under community control and, at the very least, serve the needs of the communities.

4.3.1 Group A responses

Jeannie Bell talks about the 1984 Annual General Meeting of the Australian Linguistic Society (ALS), which she attended at the Institute for Aboriginal Development in Alice Springs. At that meeting the linguistic rights of Aboriginal and Torres Strait Islander communities were workshopped and the outcome was a set of motions and statements[12] that were then endorsed by the ALS. Reflecting on that workshop, Bell says:

> I think really that people lost sight of that and Aboriginal and Torres Strait Islander community people or scholars that are doing linguistics, they feel in some ways obliged to remind the non-Indigenous linguist … 'have you thought about things this way?'

---

12   www.als.asn.au

Bell says that, in fact, she does not see any real meaningful progress since that first meeting more than 30 years ago and that Indigenous people have to keep our focus on the issues and find our own creative ways to work out the solutions for ourselves:

> We need people like yourself to keep us going with all this stuff because if we rely on all of the different organisations that we are supposedly getting support from … we might just have to be more dependent on our own creative ways really.

Jaky Troy points out that many non-Indigenous linguists approach linguistics from a scientific perspective, which has no real value on the ground to Indigenous communities who are watching their languages rapidly go to sleep:

> In some ways, linguistic research has been about not caring whether or not a community is going to keep speaking a language or not, it's been about document it before it disappears, so instead of linguists actively engaging in the future of our languages, a lot of linguists have in the past been invested in documenting languages before they die out.

Unfortunately, this is still predominantly the case and Indigenous communities are now becoming aware of the fact that documentation of a language alone does not save a language from going to sleep. Linguists argue, and rightly, that the data collected during a documentation project can then be used to teach the language in maintenance programs in the communities. However, the majority of Indigenous languages that have survived, against the odds, in Australia are severely endangered and many Indigenous communities are keenly aware that when their last speakers die, the language and the cultural knowledge will go with them. Indigenous communities in this position have often had a number of linguists come and do documentation work over many years and they have grammars and dictionaries, but they do not have a new generation of speakers coming through. Language centres have sometimes restricted linguistic research in their communities in order to find their own ways of dealing with saving their languages and, to them, it seems that non-Indigenous linguists' goals do not match the communities' goals of creating new generations of speakers.

Importantly, Vicki Couzens talks about the value of those early documentation efforts of her language in the context of revival:

> The first one is the recording, now we've got the language and for me the priority that I'm working on is grammar, rebuilding grammar, because I can have 10,000 words in my vocabulary and if I don't have grammar, I can't string them together and talk, I can't speak, I can't converse, I can't communicate; all I can say is the tree, heads shoulders knees and toes.

I would not argue that there is no great value in documenting a language, but with the rapid rate of language loss, we can no longer prioritise language documentation over language maintenance and revival efforts. To do so will see more and more languages going to sleep and language centres becoming cemeteries for Indigenous languages. Jeannie Bell points out that many Indigenous people now are asserting the right to do things their own way:

> take central Australia for instance, there are still a number of people who are fully literate in their own language, literate as well as speaking their own language and they are very strong in the sense of saying 'well we want to do it this way, we don't want you to tell us what we want'.

However, Indigenous communities in remote areas of Australia that have not yet become aware of the issues outlined here are particularly vulnerable. Some communities have no formal representative body that advocates for them and through which information can flow. These communities are often in a state of continuous crisis at multiple levels, have not had access to adequate education and experience low levels of literacy. These Indigenous communities are disempowered and vulnerable but nevertheless are often involved in linguistic research because it is often the case that in these isolated communities, the language still persists precisely because of the isolation. This was the case with my own community in western New South Wales.

Jeannie Bell talks about this vulnerability and points out that some non-Indigenous linguists continue to take advantage of the close relationships they have formed with the Indigenous people they are working with:

> then there's these other people that come along and say, 'Oh look I just need this because I've got to do this presentation and I really need you to come' and so on and, the people do it because they've been friends with them for a long time and people get used, really. They sort of like to think that it's OK because they've been around this community for a long time.

She says that while some Indigenous people are strong and will speak out, others are not so strong in this situation and the feelings of powerlessness seem overwhelming:

> It's kind of a funny situation really because people would like to be able to be strong enough to say, 'Well no you can't do that and this is the way we want to do it and we want you to do it our way'. They are just not maybe strong enough.

I am forever grateful that documentation of my language took place because it is now the only record that we have of our language. I often wonder, however, what if, instead of documentation or as well as documentation, intensive efforts were made to keep my language from going to sleep, and to create new speakers? Would I now be able to speak my language or learn from someone else who, through such efforts, had learned the language? I was a teenager at the time the documentation project was being undertaken so it would have been very feasible. It would mean so much more to me than having a grammar and a dictionary and a bunch of recordings, all of which I now have to decipher through the technical language of linguistics to have access to in any meaningful way. This is the case for all Indigenous communities who have had any documentation work done on their languages.

Importantly, Jaky Troy says that the first step is helping Indigenous people to deeply understand what linguistic research and research generally is about and how it can help their communities, and then working with them to define and develop their own research agendas:

> Ask Aboriginal and Torres Strait Island people, what are the big issues facing you and what sort of research do you want done? Do you have a sense of what research actually is and what it can do for you? And, do you understand what it does for the people who come and do research with you? I think universities need to offer themselves up in the way that I am offering up Sydney University and saying, 'Look, it's a public institution, you own it, your taxes are paying for it, paying for us to exist and if we are going to do research, it should be what you want.'

Vicki Couzens agrees and talks about actively engaging universities to negotiate Indigenous people's research agendas:

> We need to be asking communities what kind of research they want; we need to maybe direct our graduates into areas of interest that communities have prioritised. There are so many different

> levels of research and sometimes I think that it's all very well for the graduate people to have these brainiac ideas because this is so interesting. Communities need to have a research plan and priorities; wouldn't that be good if we had a research plan and priorities so that when the students come out or we can go to the university and start head-hunting people who are looking [to work with communities].

Again, Couzens agrees with Troy here about the need for communities to develop a deep understanding of research and then to formulate their own research agendas, and emphasises that non-Indigenous linguists need to help in the first instance by addressing these priorities:

> But the work needs to be done in communities around what are their research priorities, what is research? Why do we do it? What are our priorities and how are we going to do that research and with who? So, priority research. We need Master Apprentice stuff before these old people leave us and, the geeky technical stuff, we can see the importance of it structurally within the language and knowing what it is, but right now, you need to focus on this and in your spare time look at that other stuff, but the same terms and conditions still apply to all aspects of the research project.

Importantly, Couzens talks about prioritising language learning strategies such as the master apprentice program, which emphasises passing on language 'breath to breath', speaker to learner in Indigenous communities. Couzens also talks about capacity building through research projects. She says it is important for non-Indigenous linguists to be working with appropriate and interested Indigenous community members to pass on research skills and linguistic knowledge, and that this is a two-way relationship. The Indigenous linguist, language worker or community member would act as a mentor to the non-Indigenous linguist to help them to understand how the community operates and the appropriate lines of authority:

> I think the other thing that really needs to be built in [to research projects] is capacity building in community and working with community knowledge and expertise. So, if there is a community linguist, someone who's been doing the work but not formal-education trained, they must work with these people, they must understand the lines of authority in community and how it all works and training people up, not that they [the linguist] have to deliver the training per se, some of it might be on the job, but be there to be part of handing on skills and knowledge to the community.

85

When thinking about how Indigenous communities might be able to promote their critical research agenda to interested researchers, Vicki Couzens imagines some sort of database in the future that could match up communities' research agendas with university graduates looking for communities to work with:

> What if we had a database where people logged on, and we had like a linguist and community projects, a love match [database]. It could be online perhaps with First Languages Australia.

In light of the fact that significant meaningful change in linguistic practice within the academy in Australia has been painstakingly slow, a group of Indigenous linguists and language activists have formed the Alliance of Indigenous Linguist Research (AILR) in order to take a leading role in the protection and promotion of Indigenous people's rights in linguistics research. In its founding document, AILR states:

> Moving on from this seminal ALS meeting and the pioneering work of Jeannie Bell, we have decided to form a permanent group, the Indigenous Alliance for Linguistic Research, to further her important contribution to the field. It is our intention to decolonise the discipline of linguistics and claim it for Indigenous people. We intend to no longer be the 'subjects' of linguistic research but to be recognised for the researchers that we already are and making valuable contributions to the discipline.

At the time of writing, AILR is still in the very formative stages, but it is planned to formally organise the group in the near future. This is a very positive move for Indigenous people's linguistic rights in Australia and one that is in line with Indigenous groups in other parts of the world such as North America and New Zealand.

4.3.2 Group B responses

> The new ethics have developed in large part due to the demands by the communities themselves, as they emerge from generations of genocide and oppression, and begin to exercise their own rights of decision making.
>
> Leanne Hinton (2010, p. 35)

Encouragingly, some non-Indigenous linguists are beginning to listen deeply to what Indigenous people have been saying and are taking measures to work in genuinely collaborative ways with Indigenous people to begin to redress some of the issues on both sides. It must be noted that much of this work is happening outside of the academy. Margaret Florey talks about the underlying principles of the DRIL, and professional development training programs run through RNLD/Living Languages, and says the core principles are twofold: helping Indigenous people to better understand the field of linguistics generally, and being able to undertake their own linguistic and language work or engage with non-Indigenous linguists in an empowered way. She says:

> I think that training is an important part of it, that as community people get a better understanding of linguistics and the work that linguists do and it opens up that possibility of one of them being able to do it themselves, but also it opens up the confidence to know a linguist could come and do this and we might stand a chance of understanding what they are doing and if we want to still maintain control, we might still be able to do that. So, it puts people in a stronger position to being able to ask us the question or ask someone else the question, 'that'd be really good for us, do you know somebody who might be able to come in and do this?' Because I think in the early stages people just haven't got a clue what they might even be asking for or what might come out of that. I think there's absolutely that value of trying to do that bridging and that match-making service.

Felicity Meakins also talks about the role that language centres can play in being a bridge between Indigenous communities and universities around negotiating community directed research:

> I think that's where really good relationships between language centres and universities are really powerful; the linguists in the language centre were the ones who were on the ground talking to community members and they'd be saying 'we want this' and then we could communicate that to universities, and the linguists in universities often have more funding pull and that sort of thing.

Margaret Florey and Kris Travers Eira say that RNLD/Living Languages and VACL also do that bridging between university graduates and Indigenous communities. However, Amy Parncutt, a young non-Indigenous linguist who was working with RNLD/Living Languages at the time of my research, warns that if Indigenous people rely too heavily on this model, they risk becoming dependent on non-Indigenous linguists in the university system to do their language and linguistic work for them:

> You also don't want to, if there are stronger partnerships between language centres and universities, then you also run that risk of it going back to thinking, 'this is the only option for my language to get documented—I need a white linguist to come in, that's how it's done' rather than going, 'oh I can actually do this myself'.

The point that Parncutt makes here is critical; while Indigenous people do want to build stronger and more productive relationships with universities to help them address the issues within their own communities, it must not be the case that these relationships would undermine Indigenous people's aspirations to maintain control and ownership of research or projects that take place in their communities, and which deal with their languages and cultural knowledge.

While there is a genuine desire by Indigenous people to manage and control research projects, there is currently a severe lack of resources that would help Indigenous people do this effectively in their communities and organisations. In the past several years, funding cuts to the federal government's Indigenous languages budget have seen language centre funding cut severely, leaving most language centres with greatly reduced staff. However, in 2021, the federal government announced $22.8 million in new funding for Indigenous languages 'as part of the Commonwealth Implementation Plan for Closing the Gap'.[13] The announcement says that the funding will include additional support for existing language centres and the establishment of three new language centres. It is not clear yet if this is ongoing funding, but it will be a welcome boost to language centres' capacity to operate. Importantly, Jess Soller, a young non-Indigenous linguist who was working with RNLD/Living Languages at the time of this research, talks about the extra responsibility that comes with making sure research is carried out in an ethical manner: who has that responsibility and will non-Indigenous linguists need some special training? She says:

> I suppose then there's a responsibility for the language centres to make sure that the linguists that are going to come in are going to work in a relatively ethical and good way; whether that requires them have to do extra training with the linguist in that language centre or whether they are going to have to have a relationship and negotiation where students are coming from, to make sure they are trained in an appropriate way.

---

13   www.firstlanguages.org.au/news

4. WHAT DID THEY SAY?

Kris Travers Eiera says that graduate linguists coming out of university are often ill-equipped to be working in Indigenous communities. They say that universities teach students how to 'do' linguistics but not 'how' to be a linguist working in Indigenous communities and this has often resulted in a breakdown in research projects:

> the lack of preparation of the grad students for the realities of working in communities and, my friend in academia who I keep referring to, she went for something like three months' fieldwork and came back with something like an hour of data, that's the reality.

The issues raised here by Soller and Kris Travers Eira are not to be overlooked; if the non-Indigenous linguist has no or little understanding of what the issues are, then going unprepared into an Indigenous community can do more harm than good—to both the Indigenous community and the non-Indigenous linguistic community as a whole.

Everyone I spoke to said that they had had no training around the issue of ethics in linguistic research in their undergraduate or postgraduate training, and only one participant undertook a course in fieldwork methods, which she felt had not prepared her for the reality she faced on the ground in communities. Parncutt talks about feeling like she had been given a solid grounding in the issues in her undergraduate studies but when she started working at RNLD in the DRIL training program and hearing what the issues really are for Indigenous people on the ground around Australia, she realised that the training she had received was still missing the mark:

> when I was at university, I really thought that a lot of my lecturers, like that that was the training you know. It did seem so community focussed from some of my classes, so I really thought that that was, you know the way to work with Indigenous people and they were doing the right thing by community, but it's no, until you come to this space and then it's like 'oh you think you are but really, you're still not'.

I believe it is the responsibility of universities to properly educate graduates around the issues of ethics and particularly the critical importance of 'free, prior and informed consent' and how that feeds into the development of robust agreements in the context of working with Indigenous people. This of course implies a solid period of consultation with the community to work through these issues. As Parncutt points out, even the fieldwork courses that are being delivered (and I believe there are only a couple of universities offering these) fall short of the realities and expectations of Indigenous people on the ground in communities.

Currently, the opportunities are very few for non-Indigenous graduate linguists to gain the necessary skills and experience around these issues. RNLD/Living Languages' practice of taking young graduates out into Indigenous communities is clearly a very good—and perhaps the only—model in Australia that truly strives to address the issues in a meaningful way, aiming to meet the needs of Indigenous people and strengthen relationships between the two groups. Some language centres have had and continue to have interns and volunteers working with their organisations, such as Ngukurr Language Centre in the Northern Territory, Mirima Dawang Woorlab-gerring Language and Culture Centre and Wangka Maya Pilbara Aboriginal Language Centre in Western Australia, which is also a good model for exposing young graduate linguists to working with Indigenous communities and experiencing first-hand the realities on the ground.

However, universities ultimately have the responsibility to deliver targeted courses for working with Indigenous communities based on sound ethics guided by and developed in conjunction with Indigenous people. As previously stated, I believe that AIATSIS as the peak organisation that represents Indigenous people's rights in research broadly, has a strong role to play in partnering with universities to ensure that graduates intending to work in Indigenous communities, at the very least, meet the requirements of the AIATSIS Code of Ethics, through a mandatory online course or some other instrument.

4.4 The issues and moving forward together

> It really is a very big undertaking because this is a post-colonial country we are still wrestling with; how do we be with each other? It's not easy and it's not going to be easy, no matter what you do, that's at the heart of what the difficulties are around ethics and protocols in Australia that as we know, on a broader scale and outside of linguistics totally, that's still not really acknowledged in Australia, but we are getting there and so within linguistics, same. It's not acknowledged how hard that is and why, and what the hell you do about it.
>
> Kris Travers Eira, Interview, 2016

Kris Travers Eira reflects here on what I would consider to be core to the reasons why, to date, there have been no concerted efforts to see what progress we've made in linguistics since that first meeting in 1984.

It's seen to be too difficult, too political and, indeed, it is very difficult and very political on both sides, but nonetheless, there is willingness to try again and to keep trying to work through the issues in small pockets around the country. The work that RNLD/Living Languages and VACL do is a clear demonstration of this willingness, and there are also many language projects that continue to try really hard to get the balance right for all concerned.

Despite this, there has been no forum dedicated to the issues since the meeting in Alice Springs in 1984. Jeannie Bell, who was at that meeting and has worked actively with communities and universities to bring light to the issues since that time, feels that nothing has changed:

> It just makes you feel real sad really, you know because we have all done our time protesting and doing all of that sort of stuff and nothing much changes.

4.4.1 What are the issues for Indigenous linguists and practitioners?

> Everybody doing linguistics in Australia should be doing something to build the future for our languages and all the other side of it can wait or can be done as a side issue. Any documentation should have built into it an active aspect of keeping a language going, the main object is to get people invested in keeping our languages going. Our languages should be part of our future, not part of our past.
>
> Jaky Troy, Interview, 2016

Jaky Troy hits on a major ongoing concern for many Indigenous people around Australia whose languages are severely endangered, that is 'saving' languages from going to sleep and prioritising language maintenance and revival strategies that ensure the next generation are learning their languages 'breath to breath'. The KLRC have been saying this for some time now and they have restricted documentation in their area because they say that documentation alone does not save their languages. While non-Indigenous linguists are also deeply concerned about the critical rate that Indigenous languages have been going to sleep and documentation is a major priority for them, the reality is that there is no concerted effort on the part of non-Indigenous linguists to help keep severely threatened languages alive and on the tongues of the speakers. The major concern of many non-Indigenous linguists is to create a grammar and perhaps a dictionary of the language before the last speakers die, which is then given back to the communities in the form of texts that they cannot read unless they then undertake some linguistic training to decode. This is in large part due to the structure of universities and major funding agencies. This was discussed in Section 2.9 in Chapter 2.

Indigenous people want to be in control of research projects and are beginning to push back and say they no longer want to be treated as the 'subjects' of scientific research and, if non-Indigenous linguists want to work with them, then they will have to work to Indigenous people's own research agendas. Jaky Troy says:

> I don't think this country can sustain a model where people come in and do research with our people into the future that isn't going to serve the purposes of the communities that research is being done with; so that should be the starting point, not someone has a bright idea they want to understand some aspect of the verbal morphology of Pama-Nyngan languages—and that's a valid thing to do—but if you are going to go and do research in a community, get access to that kind of information, go and find out what the community wants done first and do a PhD on that, and if you want write some navel-gazing piece into the future when you've learnt about the language, do it later on.

This situation puts non-Indigenous linguists and Indigenous communities in a very real bind. Some non-Indigenous linguists are critical of Indigenous communities and organisations that choose to restrict documentation because, in part, this could negatively impact their field and their careers. Further, major funding organisations' narrow views on what constitutes research are out of touch with Indigenous people's growing concerns and awareness of the ethics in linguistic research. Linguists are now beginning to see and experience how this situation is becoming unworkable on the ground in more and more Indigenous communities and organisations. Many Indigenous people have little sympathy or desire to continue to engage with non-Indigenous linguists on these issues. Troy speaks plainly and says:

> I hate to say it, but I've got no sympathy for linguists feeling threatened, I actually think that that's part of the colonial process. I don't think that linguists should have any privilege in the process at all, it's a privilege to be a linguist working on an Australian language. It should be 'we are the dog, they are the tails; I am a linguist in a linguist role, I'm the tail not the dog, and I need to take direction from the people I'm working with for the purposes that those people identify, and all the academic navel-gazing stuff can go on but not as the primary exercise'. Our languages are going to disappear and someone getting a PhD on some esoteric aspect of linguistics is a waste of three years' worth of Commonwealth research funding.

Vicki Couzens says that she is exhausted by the ongoing battle to have Indigenous people's issues addressed in the field of linguistics and that her energies now will be focussed on her own family and her own community and doing things her way. She says:

> I have less energy and I am less inclined to expend a lot of my energy jumping up and down and screaming and shouting and banging my head against the colonial brick wall anymore. I'm not going to spend the next thirty years of my life trying to educate the white man; I'm going to spend that in my community and my family.

Jeannie Bell notes that when Indigenous linguists and activists speak out and try to make some inroads or bring attention to matters of concern for Indigenous people, they are often criticised, questioned, or put down by non-Indigenous linguists. She talks about Jaky Troy being a strong advocate and warrior for our people:

> I don't know because the Indigenous linguists are getting fewer and fewer that are doing actual teaching at universities, there's not many is there? Jaky Troy for instance, she spent all that time in Sydney then back in Canberra and she's always been trying to get things happening but people put her down all the time; like somebody said when I told someone when she got the job at Sydney University, and she went, 'how come she gets that job?' and I'm thinking well what hell has it go to do with you, why do you have to go like that? She's had her PhD for how many damn decades and people just think it's OK to run her down because she doesn't work things like you do.

I can relate to what Bell is saying here. I have had similar experiences myself and felt at times that some non-Indigenous linguists have felt threatened by my presence in the workplace or at conferences because of my activism. I have often been sidelined, ignored or actively undermined by some non-Indigenous linguists in the past. This situation can make it incredibly hard for Indigenous linguists and language activists to maintain enthusiasm to continue to work in the field of linguistics, and, as previously mentioned, perhaps that is why so many Indigenous people do not actively go on to pursue a career in linguistics.

Jaky Troy points out that part of the problem lies with linguists' often overinflated ideas about linguistics and the belief that only highly intelligent people can engage in the field. She says:

> There's been a very much kind of 'us and them' approach in the field. I think that linguists need to be a lot less arrogant and of course it's not everybody, but there is still a real arrogance in the linguistic world; that it is a difficult field of study, that only people who are highly intellectual can engage with, and that actually cuts out the idea that the communities that the people are working with are actually highly intellectual, producing materials and information in their own way about their languages and training the linguists, but that's not recognised.

The idea that Indigenous people are not intelligent and could not understand or engage with linguistics is extremely arrogant and deeply rooted in the fictitious notion that Western or global knowledge systems are superior. Vietnamese Australian researcher Chi Luu[14] says:

> There are many ways of seeing the world, and indigenous cultures all around it have had a long time to amass a great knowledge about how things work. They have evolved languages to tell people about it in ways that they could understand. By mistaking a culture's hard won history for a fantasy, or by disrespecting the wealth of knowledge in all its different forms, treating it as worthless because it doesn't look like the conventions we expect, we're merely keeping up a Columbian, colonial tradition of treating people not like ourselves as less than human. And that might cost us more than we expect.

---

14   daily.jstor.org/daily-author/chi-luu/

Linguistics itself is not a complicated field per se; it is only the way in which it is presented, couched in tediously pompous language that makes it hard to comprehend. I would recommend that linguistics move to a plain language model, as is being advocated for in the legal profession in the United States.[15]

Troy goes on to say that currently there are no spaces in linguistics in Australia where Indigenous and non-Indigenous linguists, language workers and activists get together to share their knowledge about languages and their shared work:

> I still see at the Australian Linguistics Society, there's the forum for the Aboriginal and Torres Strait Islander people and then the forum for the linguists, there doesn't seem to be a real marrying up. I don't think it's a matter of having Aboriginal and Torres Strait Islander people qualified in linguistics; it's about having that discussion that happens in the field, where people do understand each other and giving that a privileged in the space in linguistics. Aboriginal people do do linguistics or linguists wouldn't be able to write anything. We share our knowledge about our languages with linguists and linguists then go away and take that and divorce us from that sharing moment.

This divorcing of Indigenous people whose languages are being presented and discussed at conferences assumes that Indigenous people will not understand or be interested in what is being presented, and, where linguistics is presented in turgid language, that only people with any training in linguistics might have a chance of understanding. This practice alienates Indigenous people from the linguistic work in which they were initially a 'vital' collaborator. Further, this practice continues to perpetuate Indigenous people as subjects of scientific research.

Troy says that many Indigenous organisations, including language centres, are beginning to reject non-Indigenous linguists. She says that researchers from the social sciences generally have been seen to be predominantly concerned with their own careers at the expense of the Indigenous communities they have been working in:

---

15   www.plainlanguage.gov/resources/content-types/legal-profession/

> In some ways, the peak national bodies, both FATSIL[16] and now First Languages Australia, are almost anti-linguist, which is a real problem. I think that what's happened is that anthropology, linguistics, and archaeology as well, these social sciences are seen to be the fly-in-fly-out sort of model, even if people have come for some years to develop their knowledge of a language and then write up a grammar, it's seen as a come-and-take and then go-away-and-put-nothing-back exercise. So, I think longevity of engagement.

Long-term meaningful collaboration is crucial; it is no longer acceptable to divorce Indigenous people from all aspects of their languages and cultural knowledges in the research context beyond fieldwork, as is still the case in the majority of linguistic research in Australia. Many non-Indigenous linguists do maintain long-term relationships with the community in which they have been undertaking their research, but this does not always equate to a meaningful collaboration beyond the fieldwork or the extraction of knowledge. This is precisely why we are seeing an anti-linguist push back from Indigenous people and it is why we are seeing Indigenous organisations and language centres insisting on using agreements to counter some of these problems.

In the language revival context, which is now the situation in the majority of Australia, Indigenous people feel that some non-Indigenous linguists in the academy devalue language revival efforts and fail to recognise the absolute struggle that Indigenous people are facing when trying to revive their languages and what it actually means to them. This suggests that only spoken languages are of any real interest to non-Indigenous linguists and, in many cases, this bears out in practice. Further, many non-Indigenous linguists are often not interested in helping Indigenous communities keep their languages on their tongues but only in documenting the language before the last speaker dies and producing a grammar and a dictionary. By and large, this comes back to issue of the very narrow view of what constitutes valid research and what attracts research funding.

Simon Musgrave and Nick Thieberger say that the work of language revitalisation for Indigenous communities is about 'language affection' and for non-Indigenous linguists interested in the scientific study of languages, this kind of work is 'thin and unsatisfying' (2007, p. 49).

---

16 First Languages Australia (formerly FATSIL) is the national peak body for all Aboriginal and Torres Strait Islander languages. www.firstlanguages.org.au/about

The rhetoric being used in papers such as this is now being challenged by many Indigenous linguists and activists and is seen as devaluing and unacceptable. Jenny Davis (2017) has dedicated a whole article to this problem and I would highly recommend this article to all non-Indigenous linguists. Further, Jaky Troy says:

> People like John Hobson who are actually quite critical, saying that some communities only want to use the language for symbolic purposes; well that perhaps is because that's the only way forward that they can see, but if they can understand what's involved in reviving a language and speaking it again and having your kids growing up learning the language, let's have communities really well informed about the state of our languages and what we can do into the future to make sure that we, as Aboriginal people, will be speaking Aboriginal languages. That's the big question, how do we as Aboriginal people carry ourselves forward into the future speaking our own languages?

Troy goes on to say that all linguists working on Australian languages should be activists for our languages because we are losing them at an alarming rate:

> Most of our languages only have a few fluent speakers now, there are only thirteen that are still really strong and are widely used in communities, so we are in a pretty desperate situation and there needs to be a better way of transmitting our languages into the future and growing them, and linguists actually should all be activists.

The non-Indigenous linguistic community has a strong role to play in advocating for changes to research funding that would argue for the value of applied strategies that identify, investigate and offer solutions to the real-life problems of helping Indigenous people do the work of saving and revitalising our languages. Troy says that Indigenous and non-Indigenous people can, in this process, get their degrees, but there needs to be a much more collaborative way forward.

Collaboration must begin well before ethics applications or research begins and this must be factored into a research project. I would recommend at least six months' lead-up time. The Indigenous people involved in language documentation and other types of linguistic research must be involved in all stages of research planning and development, project management, language analysis, the development of theories and in the presentation of research findings, including theses and publications.

In short, Indigenous people must be seen as fully human, intelligent and capable of being equal partners in all aspects of research that involves or is about them.

4.4.2 What are the issues for non-Indigenous linguists?

> Why should Indigenous people try and put their energy there when their energy is needed for the revitalisation side of things, and I think that those issues of authority come into this as well, that if people are fearful of what might happen if people have control over their own language programs, a response to that is, if we are trying to build appropriate and respectful relationships there won't be anything to fear, because appropriate and respectful relationships will look to the needs of all parties and see how we can address them.
>
> Margaret Florey, Interview, 2016

The work that is being undertaken by Living Languages and the organisation's underlying ethos are definitely to be applauded. It is an organisation that has listened deeply to what Indigenous people are saying and has taken active steps to build strong and respectful relationships with Indigenous peoples and their communities.

Margaret Florey, co-founder of the RNLD and director of its Documenting and Revitalising Indigenous Languages training program, talks about how non-Indigenous linguists need to be thinking about what is happening on the ground around Australia with the destruction of Indigenous languages and working hand in hand with Indigenous people and their communities to begin to address some of the issues identified above. She says:

> I think Aboriginal people are hearing that there's no hope for our languages so there's this sort of push to document and archive so that we've got the material, because they are not going to live, rather than taking from the perspective of 'if our starting point is well what can we be doing to sort of stop that process of the destruction and really support the languages living now and do

> the documentation hand in hand, there's no reason why you can't be documenting MA sessions and doing that enterprise side by side' and I think that's just incredibly vital.

Importantly she talks about RNLD's role in inducting young graduate linguists into the Indigenous communities around Australia to help them get first-hand experience of the issues on the ground around what it means to work in Indigenous communities and build an understanding of what linguistics is and what are benefits of good collaborative linguistic research for Indigenous people:

> getting hold of the young linguists as we try and do at RNLD and take them to workshops in their formative years and really get them to be able to sit down face to face with Aboriginal people and talk about what the needs are from both sides.

With more and more Indigenous people and communities asserting that they want to have control over research and projects that concern or are about them, there is a growing tension between Indigenous people and communities and non-Indigenous linguists. Florey says many non-Indigenous linguists have at the forefront of their mind the idea that if Indigenous people have control over their own research and projects, their own careers will be negatively impacted, and that if Indigenous people are not researchers themselves, how will they understand what linguists do?

> [H]ow are they going to meet publishing demands, how are they going to meet their research goals if they are having to be concerned about this and, if somebody else has authority over their project, will they be allowed? ... The fear of what are they going to stop us from doing rather than what are they going to allow us from doing [to be doing]. The onus there now is on the non-Indigenous researchers to find a way to help people understand what their projects are about and what the benefit might be not just to science.

This fear is very real for non-Indigenous linguists. They fear that they will have to enter into contracts with Indigenous people that stipulate what can and can't be done with the research results and that such contracts will be overly restrictive compared to the current situation. The prospect of having to renegotiate every new publication or use of the research results might mean that the linguist—Indigenous or non-Indigenous—may have to visit the Indigenous community again; this can be time consuming, and it does not guarantee the desired outcome. But, as Florey points out, the onus is on the linguist to find ways of helping the Indigenous community clearly understand what the proposed publication or presentation is about and, critically, whether they can co-author or co-present with their co-researchers, and what happens to the copyright of any proposed new publication.

Non-Indigenous linguists need to take into account that Indigenous communities are in a state of constant crisis at so many levels and those communities that still have their languages are often faced with the knowledge that their language is in a critical state of endangerment. This is true of the majority of languages still spoken in Australia. There is very little room in the lives of Indigenous people to be concerned for the careers of non-Indigenous linguists if they are seen to be not in line with Indigenous people's own agendas. Florey agrees and says:

> I remember at CoLang[17] when I was taking part in the 'Life in Communities' workshop and a couple of the non-Indigenous people were talking about those demands, and one of my responses to that was, 'well why do you think that Indigenous people should care about your career path and prioritise your career path over what they need to do for their community?' There was a ripple of shock through the room when I said it because I think that still there's this kind of feeling that this is our reality, we have to be able to publish a couple of papers a year, we have to be able to do this kind of research and I think there has traditionally been an expectation that everyone will understand that and will work with it and I think that we are at a crossroads there.

If research is aligned with the Indigenous communities' own identified priorities and identified Indigenous people within the community are engaged as co-researchers, there is a much greater chance that the research will be supported in an ongoing manner and, therefore, a much higher likelihood of the project being successful. I am currently undertaking a PhD program, and this is the premise of my own research. I have prioritised broad community consultation at all stages of the project including well before taking up my PhD program. I conduct regular visits to the communities outside of fieldwork. I have six Indigenous co-researchers from within my own community working alongside of me and I keep the broader community up to date with the progress of the project through a dedicated Facebook page. While I did not enter into a research agreement

---

17   www.colanginstitute.org

for the project, I did ensure that all of the co-researchers maintained the copyright in their data through the instrument of consent forms that give me permission to use their data only for the PhD project. All other future uses will have to be negotiated with them. This is expected from my community. It is critical to my project that I have and continue to maintain the community's trust and support.

The growing awareness of Indigenous people has caused a shift in the dynamics of the relationships between Indigenous people and non-Indigenous linguists, and this has the effect of creating ambivalence and uncertainty for many non-Indigenous linguists who actively engage in the agenda of returning control and authority to Indigenous people within their own practices. Kris Travers Eira says that it is perceived that the knowledge and skills they bring to the table are undervalued:

> I guess a pendulum swing the other way so that knowledge and skills that I bring are disregarded or not wanted. I recognise that that's just pendulum swing, that's what that is, it is pretty frustrating; that's where we are.

Conversely, Felicity Meakins talks about the emotional trauma of being a non-Indigenous linguist working in Indigenous communities. She says that many non-Indigenous linguists feel a deep sense of guilt surrounding the colonial history of this country and she questions the right of non-Indigenous linguists to be working in Indigenous communities. She says that this can be a factor in the tensions that exist between non-Indigenous linguists and Indigenous people:

> there's a lot of guilt, I think most non-Indigenous linguists are pretty left-leaning in terms of politics and just know all of the problems that's gone on over the past couple of centuries and so there's an awful lot of guilt associated with that. Then there's a sense that a lot of us that it's not our place to be working in this space; for instance, as a woman in this day and age, if you had men studying women or men running women's organisations there'd be outcry about that … So, I guess often as a non-Indigenous linguist you're thinking well this isn't really my place to be undertaking language work and when an Indigenous linguist calls you out on something, it hits at all that feeling of unease that you already have and I think that maybe that's why people get their backs up, because they're wanting to do the right thing.

Many Indigenous people say that the guilt of non-Indigenous linguists is a part of the colonial process, as are the continued unethical practices of linguistic research. I think that when the field of linguistics engages in genuinely ethical practice, then this situation will eventually be resolved. Kris Travers Eira talks about how we are still struggling with how to move forward together and how hard the process is and the fact that it is not really acknowledged.

Many Indigenous people would argue that we are not in a post-colonial country: colonial rule is still deeply experienced by Indigenous people. Australia is one of the few countries in the Commonwealth that does not have a treaty with its Indigenous peoples and there is, to date, no recognition of Indigenous people in Australia's constitution. Kris Travers Eira talks explicitly about the very uncomfortable space that we find ourselves in with Indigenous people pushing back and articulating the need for urgent change to redress the human rights concerns in linguistic research, and with non-Indigenous linguists struggling to work out what this means for them and how they will address the requirements of their institutions. This situation is complex and difficult on both sides and has at times caused considerable tension between the groups.

Many Indigenous people are becoming strong and outspoken leaders in their own organisations and asserting their rights around research that takes place in their communities. This move has drawn some criticism from some non-Indigenous linguists such as Musgrave and Thieberger who question their authority and say that some Indigenous people have little sympathy for the aims of linguists (2007, p. 50). Margaret Florey says that some linguists are fearful of working in organisations where there is strong Indigenous leadership:

> I do hear from linguists who hear about some language centres who have strong Indigenous leaders, and they sound fearful of those places and well 'We probably can't go there; it's going to be hard for us to work there'. I think strong Indigenous leadership is what's needed, you know, don't be scared of it, let's celebrate it, let's have those conversations, go there, and talk to people. Maybe there are regulations that people are putting in and they're asking you to sign agreements about how your work takes place, that's not a bad thing.

Non-Indigenous linguists are used to being the authority in research and this change in paradigm is unsettling. The idea that they might not be in total control of research projects leaves them feeling understandably vulnerable because they cannot see yet how this will pan out. Florey says that there is a lack of modelling in Australia about how these strongly collaborative projects might work and what they would look like. She says that there are a few in Australia that provide good models:

> In Australia, there is a lack of modelling for how that might look, I've just given some examples of a couple of projects where there are deep and lasting, very positive, relationships from both sides that are working very, very hard to meet the needs of both parties and I think they provide good models.

There are examples from the North American and New Zealand contexts among others, that describe what Indigenous-led linguistic research looks like. In the Australian context, there is much less modelling, but one recent publication in the revitalisation context *Living Languages and New Approaches to Language Revitalisation Research*, provides guidance that could be adapted to other situations (Stebbins et al., 2017). Felicity Meakins says that many non-Indigenous linguists want direction for their projects. She gives an example from a project that she has been working on:

> I think people do want direction, so the photographer I was talking about, she's Gurindji [Assoc. Prof. Brenda L Croft, The Australian National University], grew up around Sydney and Canberra and it's actually been really great working with her on projects because she's on top of all of the politics of knowledge production and ownership in ways that often community members aren't so much. It's great getting direction and insight from her which I think makes for quite a different sort of project, but she's also very gentle as well, she'll put you in your place when you've overstepped a mark and you haven't realised it, but then is encouraging, saying that the expertise that I have is appreciated on projects and certain things might not have happened if I hadn't been involved.

The situation outlined above highlights several things: it demonstrates what positive guidance can look like, but conversely, it highlights the fact there is not a lot of awareness around the issues of control and ownership of language and cultural knowledge in communities. As previously stated, this situation needs to be urgently addressed.

Meakins also points out that linguistics in the past decade has become highly technical and that this alone creates unintentional barriers and tensions:

> so, the equipment is getting harder to use, the computer programs are really hard work sometimes and I actually think the days when documentation was notebooks and pens and simple kinds of computer programs actually put up less barriers. The amount of Western education you need now to undertake these projects in ways that everybody thinks is valid is a real barrier to having the involvement of people who don't have necessarily as high a Western education, or maybe they do but they just don't have the desire to spend huge amounts of time learning computer programs when they just want to get out there and do it.

It has been my experience that Indigenous people generally have no problem with learning to use recording equipment and programs such as ELAN[18] and Audacity[19] with the right culturally appropriate training. Programs such as Toolbox[20] are more complex but again with the right training anything is possible. Some of the people that I have worked with did not achieve a high level in the Australian education system and enjoyed the challenge of learning how to use this technology to work on their own languages and produce high quality resources. Meakins goes on to say that this situation might be attracting the wrong type of non-Indigenous linguist as well as putting off Indigenous communities. She adds:

> It's becoming an expert via a Western education; language of course is something that you would always just learn as a child.

While I understand Meakins's point here and agree that becoming an expert via a Western education is not the ideal, it is where we are, and I cannot see the situation changing any time soon. Further, it would be nice to think that for all Indigenous people, learning your language as a child was the normal course of things but this is not the reality for the vast majority of Australian Indigenous people: we have to learn back our languages as second language learners. We need to engage in the national education system to access our mother tongue languages and much more.

---

18   ELAN (Computer software) (2022). Nijmegen: Max Planck Institute for Psycholinguistics, The Language Archive. archive.mpi.nl/tla/elan
19   Audacity Team (2021). Audacity(R): Free Audio Editor and Recorder (Computer application). audacityteam.org/
20   sil.org

Importantly, Meakins asks the question that she says is on the minds of some non-Indigenous linguists:

> Some non-Indigenous linguists want to know whether it is still OK to ask the bigger questions which aren't necessarily of interest to the community but are on a larger world scale and I think that's one of the things that comes up a little bit, what the interests of linguists are, some of which intersect with language communities but sometimes not, and I think maybe part of the worry is that if the goals of the community and the goals of the linguist don't overlap then is there a relationship anymore?

A response to that question could be that our goals don't always have to be the same, but they must overlap. We have seen in the data that Indigenous people are saying: 'Talk to us about our research agenda first and help us with that as a priority and work on your own interest as well but not at the expense of the community's priorities'. It may be that the Indigenous community have not yet formulated a research agenda as such, but, nevertheless, it is important to discuss the community's language priorities and the possibilities that research can offer.

Also, as previously discussed, do not assume that Indigenous people will not have an interest in the bigger questions. Find a way to talk about your research interests with the Indigenous people you are working with and see if this is something that might be of interest to them as well. If not, then they will at least know what your own research is about. Further, it is important to keep having these conversations and sharing your research interests and outcomes and looking for ongoing opportunities for collaboration.

We need to continue to work together because there is too much work that urgently needs to be done. However, non-Indigenous linguists will not have an industry in the field of Australian languages in the long term if all of our languages go to sleep, and if they cannot listen deeply and work with us to genuinely redress the inequity of human rights in linguistic research.

Some or even many linguists may choose to work on other small Indigenous languages or migrant languages from other countries, either in Australia or elsewhere, because it might be considered easier to undertake their research without having to think too much about the ethics of their research. This would not be considered a loss to Australian languages from an Indigenous point of view. Non-Indigenous linguists who embrace human rights and seek to work from a framework of shared mutual respect and dignity will always be welcome. If non-Indigenous linguists care about the loss of Australian Indigenous languages and all that they encompass, then they must listen deeply to Indigenous people and work with us to keep our languages alive or breathe new life back into them.

4.5 Creating opportunities for discussion: A way forward

> The main forum in Australia should be around what are we going to do to make sure our languages don't disappear? There is no national conference on why our languages shouldn't disappear and how to stop them disappearing. Where is the conference or the discussion where you can have community coming together with linguists and saying, 'OK let's build linguistic technique from a community perspective'?
>
> Jaky Troy, Interview, 2016

Jeannie Bell talks about the need to create opportunities for discussion of the issues between Indigenous linguists and language activists and non-Indigenous linguists (Bell, 2010, p. 92). She says the underlying tensions between the two groups need to be aired and discussed openly. She says that no space has been made for these discussions in the past 30 years and this situation continues to build resentment that can sometimes boil over at conferences when the two groups come together. I agree. There are many times that I have talked about these issues to both Indigenous and non-Indigenous linguists and language activists and yet the issues continue to get swept under the carpet because they are too sensitive, too political and are generally assigned to the 'too-hard basket'. Bell says we need to go back to that process and work out the guidelines again:

> I think that it's got to be something that people are alerted to in some sort of way, and I think the best way is that we've got to have these guidelines or whatever we are going to call them, you know like the ones that we had in the 80s.

4.5.1 Group A responses

Vicki Couzens and Jaky Troy both agree that we need to have a forum where we all get together and try again to find more equitable ways to work together. But, critically, Couzens says that Indigenous people themselves need time to discuss the issues first within their own communities:

> [We need to] go through the process and it is a process, it's not something you can sit down[and do] in an afternoon workshop; it brings up things and people need to work through their whatever it is, that emotion, that hurt or whatever it is, can be worked through and go, well, actually look, yes that's what happened then, yes that's what happened to your grandfather, the point is we're going to make sure that never happens again, so then you have the control and the authority by virtue, here's your copyright law, these are the things you can do, you've got your language reference group who are the authority that makes the decisions, this is their terms of reference and their guidelines, here's your plan on how to do your own research agenda.

Indigenous communities need to talk amongst themselves to develop a cohesive position. As we know, Indigenous people and communities are not homogenous and will have differing needs and positions. Importantly, Couzens talks about the work that the Victorian Aboriginal Corporation for Languages have put into creating a tool to help Indigenous communities facilitate discussion and work through the issues:

> Right now, we have resources to go into community or families and talk through issues, we have Meeting Point, VACL has Peetyawan Weeyn,[21] we have our new poster that we can use as tool to facilitate discussion and this is part of it, the issues if you like for want of a better word, again not reinventing the wheel either. I think that communities need to first and foremost talk among ourselves about what we want and what our positions are and then we can talk with the others, and instead of going into something and the linguist says, 'I've got this funding to come and do this research project' and someone goes, 'Oh yes great let's go and do it' and other people going no, no, no, no and then we are blueing amongst ourselves because we haven't talked through issues and we haven't done copyright, we haven't done authority and we haven't done research priorities.

---

21 Paton and Christina (n.d.).

Couzens points out that educating our own communities around the issues is an important first step; this is needed to help Indigenous people feel empowered and to be able to constructively engage in the issues, but it requires resources. She says:

> VACL through our meeting point project, we go to see different things in action and how people were going about things, but people need to feel empowered and VACL do, and we could do that so much better if we again, had the resources to get there and educate our communities.

The issue of physical and financial resources to undertake this level of consultation is no small matter. With funding cuts to the Indigenous languages budget in recent years there is little hope that this kind of large-scale project could be funded by any of the currently struggling Indigenous language centres. Vicki says that once communities have done the awareness-raising and preparation, we could then come together at a forum with non-Indigenous linguists to talk through the issues:

> Let's be prepared, let's do the preparation, talk through the issues of the frustrations around discussion of ethics, and that at a place. We might come back to and present a paper because you've done this process in the community and here's what we learnt. With what we know, maybe we have to move beyond about how things have been done before and put them forward. So, whether the community brings it up or the linguist does, someone needs to bring it up and talk about it. We've got to have it out on the table, clear the air, nut them out, draw up the ethics protocols and stuff and then we don't have to worry about it, job done.

Jaky Troy agrees and says that there needs to be a more engaged forum between the two groups and that linguists have a responsibility to be guided by what Indigenous communities have to say about linguistic research:

> Linguists haven't made a space to actually sit back and let community tell them what it is community thinks research should be. We go in with our techniques and we are not prepared to hear what it is that communities would give us guidance around, in terms of our research practices.

Vicki Couzens suggests that such a forum should be held according to Indigenous people's ideas about what such a meeting would look like. She says:

> You can bring people to a gathering that is structured and run our way and have ceremony and smoking, etc., in our space and our way; I'm sick of conferences and they are all run white people's way. You could have a space for weaving, you could have sit-down circles and so on, yes absolutely, that's a great idea, let's do it.

It is very clear from the above that there is a willingness to come together with non-Indigenous linguists to work through the issues in a constructive way. It is also clear that Indigenous communities need to first have these discussions amongst themselves in order to get up to speed on these issues and be able to put forward an informed and cohesive position. This process could take some time.

4.5.2 Group B responses

> I think that it does work; there's very few rifts that are created at CoLang,[22] very, very few. I think everyone is there with this genuine willingness and desire to just open up discussion and just throw the field open to change. It is collaborative research and everybody's really looking for this, for ways to do what you're talking about and here, it's a challenge for us in Australia.
>
> Margaret Florey, Interview, 2016

Kris Travers Eira has been committed to being open to having these difficult discussions and listening deeply to what Indigenous people have to say on the issues but says that more non-Indigenous linguists need to come to the table:

> We are going to have to accept that you can't really move through it, if you're waiting for the sun to shine it's only going to shine when we get there, we are not there, there's a lot of people carrying a lot of anger and you have to respect that.

They go on to say that currently there are very few spaces where Indigenous and non-Indigenous linguists and language activists can come together to have the difficult discussions. They say that there is no avoiding the fact that in these types of discussions, all sides will feel threatened, and we must find a way to be comfortable with being in an uncomfortable space.

---

22 The Institute on Collaborative Language Research, known as CoLang, is a biennial gathering for people to learn about language documentation, descriptive linguistics and language revitalisation. www.colanginstitute.org

Eira talks about the working relationship that they have with Couzens at VACL and how their deep trust has enabled them to have these types of discussions:

> If there are spaces to do that, they are only very very small spaces like I do with Vicki, I know that I can talk freely with Vicki and she can talk freely with me and we can have it out and that's ok, that's just her and me, it's a solid relationship there, but more publicly, we can't look for non-threatening space because it is threatening, post-colonial country, it is threatening. So maybe instead what we have to do is find spaces where it is ok to have discussion, which is in fact threatening and somehow for that to be a possible thing, not like the blowing up thing that Jeannie is referring to but you know to be uncomfortable in this bloody uncomfortable space it is.

Margaret Florey talks about the CoLang Institute on collaborative language research, and workshops such as the 'Life in Communities' course, and she reflects on how these workshops make it acceptable to confront the issues around the ethics of working with Indigenous communities in the US and from a community perspective, and to be able to ask all those questions about what it might mean for non-Indigenous linguists:

> When you're sitting in a CoLang classroom, like the 'Life in the Communities' course that I was taking part in, and you're discussing these kinds of issues where you're actually saying, like yeah what's it going to be like? People are able to ask those questions: … How would it look? How can I make it OK to come? What do I need to do? And so that, I think, confronts people on that deeper level to really think about these kinds of questions … Remembering that makes me a little bit more optimistic that I think there are these sorts of venues opening up that are making us all confront the way that we do things, but I still think in general like in Australia, if we think about, or anywhere really, if you think about a standard university classroom situation, you're too protected.

Importantly, Florey points out that universities in Australia are still white enclaves that are safe spaces for non-Indigenous people, where they do not have to move out of their comfort zone and be challenged by the reality of discussing the issues face to face with Indigenous people. She says:

> One thing that strikes me like, I think that that's part of the power of CoLang. We were talking a little bit about that earlier and I think that what strikes me about it is that, that's an environment in which you're sitting in a classroom with Indigenous people,

> non-Indigenous people, you know linguists, language workers, so everybody's mixed in there together and I think one of the great challenges is that, by and large, even if you're talking about ethical issues in a university, it's happening in a white enclave you know, and so like you're talking about it [but] you're not having to sit there and feel challenged by, in the same way that you [to Amy] say you wonder about how your research would go now thinking of like real people, real Indigenous people.

I agree with Florey here: universities are still not culturally safe spaces for Indigenous people; the balance of power is still with the non-Indigenous linguists.

Couzens's point above about having a forum or meeting that is Indigenous-led and conducted according to Indigenous ways and meeting protocols is crucial to any planned discussions. It is in this way that we can have an equal playing field and Indigenous people can feel culturally safe. Before that can happen however, Indigenous communities need to come together to discuss the issues and find their position and power in what is still very much an unequal relationship with non-Indigenous linguists. Then we can have these discussions with non-Indigenous linguists in forums that might look something like the CoLang example. When thinking about this possibility, Florey says:

> I think that they can, and I think it's to the benefit of non-Indigenous linguists to do so. Where might that forum take place and trying to get everybody to take that deep breath, and I think on both sides there's fears: Aboriginal people are fearful about sitting down in the same room with a bunch of linguists who, reasonably they might think, are going to be defensive. I think it's such an uneven table in many ways for Indigenous people, there's still too low a level of understanding of linguistics and what linguists are doing, so rightfully there's a fearfulness about what's going to happen there and for non-Indigenous people there are different levels of understanding communities and community needs and community concerns and so there's a fearfulness about that, and so how do you bridge when people aren't sitting as equals at the table?

Florey talks about the need for the Indigenous community of Indigenous linguists, language activists and language workers to meet in their own communities and places to discuss the issues before coming together:

> Maybe it needs to be a series of more regional meetings rather than one big national forum, or a regional meeting and a national forum, something like that. People are always safer on their own country or closer to their own country really letting people know [that] there is incredible goodwill and, sometimes when people say things harshly or in anger, I think it's also because they are expecting not to be heard and when they know that people are there, really with a willingness to hear and respond, then it is different, so yeah let's make it happen.

It is equally important that the non-Indigenous linguists come together in some way to have these discussions amongst themselves also. It has been my experience that there is often resistance to, or misunderstanding of, Indigenous people's concerns in this space, which has contributed to the tensions we are talking about here. There is a huge impetus here for non-Indigenous linguists to come to the table with their ideas for genuinely workable solutions to the issues.

In mid-2021 there was a very positive development in the space. A small group of non-Indigenous linguists and their affiliated universities partnered with Indigenous linguists and activists to create a forum or study group to begin to work through some of the issues:[23]

> The Indigenous Alliance for Linguistic Research, Centre of Excellence for the Dynamics of Language, Sydney Centre for Indigenous Research and the Research Unit for Indigenous Language, have formed a new study group called 'Decolonising Linguistics: Spinning a Better Yarn'. This study group aims to discuss topics of relevance to Indigenous communities involved in linguistic research and linguists more broadly, around framing a new ethical model for linguistic research based on a human rights agenda.

This study group has been well received and is still running in 2022. As this study group was set up mid-pandemic, the meetings take place online, which also makes it more accessible to people around the country wanting to attend or participate. It is planned to open the meetings to interested international audiences and participants in 2022. The sessions are recorded and are currently placed on the Centre of Excellence for the Dynamics of Language website.

---

23   legacy.dynamicsoflanguage.edu.au/index.php

While the online study group is a step in the right direction, the online format and limited time frame does not leave much room for deep discussion of the issues and certainly does not replace the need for face-to-face meetings. Kris Travers Eira says that is important to bring together people who genuinely want to resolve the issues and have a deep understanding on both sides. They suggest that this might be possible in smaller groups:

> Maybe the smaller groups thing is a key, maybe that could work, I could imagine that. Even if it was a big group like a conference, you could split it into small groups with people who on both sides and there is a both sides still, talk that through at a personal level, if you've got 400 people, you can't really talk on a personal level and sometimes that just turns to venting, and it might include people like Vicki who get both sides of the picture.

This point is crucial: both sides need to choose representatives that they trust to represent their group or community and put forward their issues in a structured and planned way. It would be unproductive to have an open forum that anyone can attend from either side because this situation could lend itself to being no more than a venting exercise. When thinking about what a forum might look like, importantly, Margaret Florey talks about the need to set a safe environment for all people involved:

> providing that safe environment for everybody and probably pre-negotiations about what are some ground rules, how do we make sure we're keeping it safe on all sides, what do we do if people stop feeling safe? Can we agree to some rules so that we can ask some hard questions but neither side is going to feel threatened? It's a good conversation for us to keep having; what would it look like?

I support Vicki Couzens's suggestion of a forum or meeting that would be based on an Indigenous model, with smoking ceremonies for healing and harmony and Indigenous ways of respectfully engaging. Margaret says that the community of non-Indigenous linguists does have a role to play in bringing the two parties together:

> I think that we are probably at a time where it is necessary and it's possible, it makes me wonder about First Languages Australia and the role that they could play. ILA [Indigenous Languages and Arts]—is it something that the ILA funding body might facilitate because it would benefit all sides? How great to set up some protocols because it's a long time since the Australian Linguistic Society created a set of rules for fieldwork but that was very much

> about if you are going to be a non-Indigenous person going into an Indigenous community 'Here's some good things to do' and, this is very different you know, this is about respectful partnerships that serve all parties.

There is enough goodwill and agreement on both sides, and it is now possible to imagine a forum where interested Indigenous linguists, activists and language workers could come together with interested non-Indigenous linguists and pick up where we left off in 1984, furthering the discussions in meaningful and lasting ways so that we can heal all that needs to be healed and move forward together. Kris Travers Eira says:

> There are people like Jeannie and yourself now as well that are bridging that gap by your work, that's got to help. Jeannie is so valuable in this area because she is just so patient and so consistent and she's always there and she does not hide her voice, she doesn't mask what she thinks but she has the respect of everybody; it's just awesome, so we could do with more Jeannies that's for sure.

We could do with more non-Indigenous linguists like Kris Travers Eira, Margaret Florey and Felicity Meakins. Unfortunately, Jeannie Bell, Margaret Florey and Kris Travers Eira have all now retired, leaving huge boots to be filled. However, it is encouraging that many young non-Indigenous linguists like Felicity Meakins are coming up through the field who believe that the human rights issues in linguistic research must be a priority and are struggling in very positive ways within their own work practices to strike the right balance.

5

Where to now?

5.1. The publish or perish dilemma: Secondary uses of research data

Up to the present, non-Indigenous linguists and researchers in other fields have had total control of research projects and research data and have published prolifically. This situation has been driven by the demands of the academy that requires academics to publish in an ongoing way to maintain their careers and continue to be able to apply for, and receive, research grants.

This situation alone has been responsible for many decades of removing Indigenous people's languages and knowledges from them and handing them over to the global scientific community. This can be likened in some ways to the removal of Indigenous artefacts and human remains to museums. However, artefacts and human remains can in most cases be repatriated: language and cultural knowledge cannot be so easily returned, and consequently much secret and sacred knowledge, among other knowledge that rightly belongs to Indigenous people, is now forever in the public domain.

In response to Indigenous people's deep concerns about how research was and still is impacting them and their knowledges, human ethics protocols for working with Indigenous people in Australia have been implemented in all universities and other government organisations involved in research. This process minimally requires researchers to 'do no harm' when researching in Indigenous communities but, to date, it does not recognise, let alone seek to redress, the 'harm' done to Indigenous people by the loss of language and cultural knowledge.

Linguistic field guides and, in my experience, ethics boards often encourage the inclusion of clauses about wide ranging, non-specific, ongoing secondary uses of language data as this facilitates unencumbered ongoing publication. The use of such clauses aims to shortcut the need for ongoing consultation with Indigenous communities that may be seen as inconvenient and time consuming.

The practice of framing ethics applications and agreements this way could be seen as a thinly veiled continuation of the exploitation of Indigenous peoples and their cultural knowledges for the purposes of scientific research.

This practice is unethical for several reasons: one, it continues to perpetuate Indigenous peoples as subjects of research; two, it denies Indigenous peoples the right to claim their knowledge as their own and to protect it in any way whatsoever; three, it denies Indigenous peoples the right to have any say in how they themselves are represented in these publications; and, lastly, it denies Indigenous peoples the opportunities to co-author publications and share in presenting their knowledges at conferences, because, critically, it assumes that Indigenous people will not understand or be interested.

Genuinely ethically informed consent must entail explaining the above situation honestly and clearly to the Indigenous people with whom the researcher intends to work.

This will require non-Indigenous linguists to find ways of talking about their proposed ongoing uses of research data, such as articles for academic journals, in ways that the Indigenous community will genuinely understand. It is no longer acceptable to say that the Indigenous community will not be interested or understand what the non-Indigenous linguist is proposing. The onus is on the non-Indigenous linguist to use plain English or the language of the community to make sure that there is a deep understanding of the proposed new uses for language data and how that data will be protected, as it must be, and to actively encourage co-authoring in such publications. This is considered best collaborative practice and is core to truly informed consent.

The use of agreements with Indigenous communities participating in research that negotiates the control of research data is now becoming seen as best practice by Indigenous people.

5.2 Indigenous control of research and use of agreements

The current ethics process in the Australian academy and AIATSIS offers no real protection for Indigenous people's knowledges and can be seen by Indigenous people as box ticking exercises. While there is strong encouragement to comply, there is no real compulsion to do so and no deterrence for not complying. In the current revised version of its ethical guidelines, AIATSIS has moved from the wording 'guidelines' to 'code' in an effort to strengthen the impact; however, this code can be interpreted as optional, with no instrument that would ensure that intended future research meets its requirements. Therefore, the Indigenous peoples of Australia are still currently vulnerable to the impacts of unethical research.

The AIATSIS code strongly encourages the use of research agreements and research partnerships, and this is a very encouraging development, but the onus is on the Indigenous community to facilitate agreements and, as pointed out above, there is still a huge gap in understanding what research actually means in many regional and remote areas of Australia. This is particularly true in communities that do not have a language centre or other cultural organisation with strong Indigenous leadership.

In organisations that do have strong Indigenous leadership, the use of agreements is becoming common practice, particularly in language centres, and this is considered to be best practice by Indigenous people. Typically, these agreements aim to keep the copyright of language and cultural knowledge with the language speakers and within Indigenous families or communities and include succession plans for copyright. These agreements usually are in the form of a licence to use language data for specific agreed outcomes, including secondary uses of data, with the expectation that non-Indigenous linguists will continue to seek, in an ongoing manner, permission for each proposed new use.

The use of agreements as outlined above should also be standard practice in linguistic research that emanates from the academy or any other organisation involved in research. While there is no compulsion to do so from ethics committees, non-Indigenous linguists must now act in 'good faith' of their own volition, according to the AIATSIS code, and actively seek to negotiate these types of agreements where ongoing control of research data would remain with the speakers. This is particularly pertinent in communities where there is no strong representation or organisation that would help them negotiate an agreement. Acknowledging that control of language and cultural knowledge in research data remains with the speakers is of crucial importance to Indigenous people's human rights. Non-Indigenous linguists are slowly coming to terms with this situation and there is a general acceptance that best ethical practice benefits the field of linguistics in the longer term.

5.3 Indigenous linguistic training and work

It is abundantly clear that Indigenous people want the skills and knowledge to be able to undertake their own linguistic and language work, and for that work to be valued and supported by the community of non-Indigenous linguists.

In light of the fact that intellectual property and copyright laws and the systems within the academy fail to protect Indigenous peoples' language and cultural knowledge, Indigenous people are best able to manage their language and cultural knowledge within their communities into the future; in this way, they themselves get to make the decisions about who has access to that knowledge and how that takes place.

Indigenous people have taken the view that if non-Indigenous linguists want to be helpful in this space, then they will actively engage in this agenda in a way that gives Indigenous people agency in whatever shared linguistic research or work that takes place together in the future. In this shifting paradigm some non-Indigenous linguists are beginning to see training and passing on linguistic skills to Indigenous people as a valid and meaningful role for them in linguistics.

Encouragingly, many research grants now require that training Indigenous people to enable them to undertake their own linguistic or other research must be a part of the outcomes of a project. This is a welcome and much needed development.

5.4 Community education of the issues

There is a huge lack of awareness within Indigenous communities around exactly how research currently operates to lock away their rights in their language and cultural knowledges with intellectual property rights actually offering no protection.

Many Indigenous communities have no representative organisation or structure that allows for the flow of information in either direction; they therefore remain vulnerable to the research that is undertaken by non-Indigenous linguists and other researchers, who believe that the current status quo in universities is acceptable.

Indigenous communities in regional and remote regions of Australia are generally unaware that the systems of the academy and the unrelenting thirst for new knowledge and knowledge production see Indigenous peoples' languages and cultural knowledge taken away from them, more often than not inadvertently, through the structure of research itself, copyright laws and the systems of publishing. This system often serves the academic needs of the researcher.

Further, there is also very little understanding that it is possible and desirable to have control over research that happens in Indigenous communities and how research can be of benefit to their own agendas, protecting Indigenous languages and knowledge and for the economic development of their communities.

This is one of our greatest shared ethical dilemmas and challenges and there is an urgent need for Indigenous communities to become educated on the issues so that they can begin to operate from a position of knowledge and power. The community of non-Indigenous linguists needs to actively work with Indigenous people to find ways to reform these systems.

5.5 Co-authoring

Many non-Indigenous linguists are struggling in very positive ways to understand and support the aspirations of Indigenous people in regaining control of their language and cultural knowledge. Co-authoring with Indigenous co-researchers is beginning to be considered as a practical way of managing copyright for the individuals involved. However, co-authoring has limited value as it does not address the larger problem of the rights of the speech community.

This is already an acceptable way to publish articles in academic journals and texts but co-authoring with Indigenous co-researchers is not yet common practice in the Australian context. Co-authoring dissertations is already a practice in the hard sciences but is not yet seen as an option in the arts and humanities, and I would recommend that this be considered as a potential model in the field of linguistics in the context of research involving Indigenous people. It has been suggested that Indigenous people involved in language documentation projects are co-researchers because they are teaching and describing their language in depth to the linguist, and this is considered joint analysis and should be recognised as such.

However, publishing with many academic journals means that the authors will lose copyright to the publisher. In this context, co-authoring does not provide any protection to Indigenous people's language and cultural knowledge, and has the effect of twice removing from Indigenous people and communities their language and the cultural knowledge contained in these types of publications.

It is recommended that non-Indigenous linguists look for publishing opportunities that do not seek to take the copyright in the article or book. If this is not possible and the article contains language and cultural information of a people, the linguist needs to negotiate this in a very honest and open way with the Indigenous community involved and respect their decisions to allow publication or not, or seek alternative publishing options.

5.6 Shared goals

Many academic linguists are locked into a system driven by the scientific search for new knowledge and a 'publish or perish' environment that many feel is out of their individual control. While this is not true for all linguists working in an academic setting, and no doubt many enjoy the process of sharing their research, publications are generally considered vital to improving their chances of receiving ongoing research funding and advancing their careers. Non-Indigenous linguists wonder how these ethics, that seem so out of kilter with the requirements of the academy and what is expected of them, will impact them in the longer term. Non-Indigenous linguists now wonder if they and Indigenous communities will still have a relationship when, on the surface, it seems so unworkable and onerous.

The onus here is on non-Indigenous linguists who want to work on Indigenous Australian languages. They must now begin to find ways in their own work practices to account for the fact that control of language and cultural knowledge is a high priority for Indigenous people. This must be factored into ethics applications, grant applications and agreements processes. Non-Indigenous linguists must also understand that consultation with and seeking permission from Indigenous communities is an ongoing process.

Linguists must also take this into account when planning their research or projects and factor in that it will take longer. This might seem inconvenient, but from an Indigenous perspective, it is crucial. I would recommend that PhD programs also be extended by at least six months to allow for ongoing community consultation.

Further, can non-Indigenous linguists genuinely say that they share the same goals as Indigenous communities in 'saving' their languages or preserving their languages for future generations if all that they offer the Indigenous community is a grammar and a dictionary—which then requires the community to understand the technical language of linguistics in order to unlock that material and, only once they have done this, can they then use these resources to re-learn their languages as second language learners, once the last speaker has died?

It is crucial that linguists now actively seek to work with Indigenous communities on their priorities in ways that give Indigenous people agency in all aspects of that work. Training for Indigenous people in linguistics and research skills is a priority and must be factored into research projects. Linguists can still undertake research in their specific interest areas, but Indigenous people are now saying that this must not happen at the expense of their language priorities and needs.

Linguistics as a field needs to urgently reform. We have seen a shift away from the traditional view of description of language through the production of a grammar, a dictionary and a set of texts, to thinking about the value of documentation to other areas of linguistic enquiry, such as language shift among many others. We now need to see a shift to the value of linguistics to Indigenous people themselves.

Non-Indigenous linguists continue to produce resources that they think will be of value to Indigenous people, but the reality is that these resources are still overly reliant on linguistic jargon, and, therefore, are difficult to understand and are of no real practical value to Indigenous people. I would include here the majority of dictionaries that are produced by linguists. Dictionaries are usually produced with other linguists as the main target audience with the hope that it will also be of some value to the Indigenous community: of course there are exceptions, but not many. More recently, we have also seen the production of learners' grammars or guides intended for the Indigenous community that are still very much couched in the technical language of linguistics, making them, unfortunately, still predominantly inaccessible.

We need to see a shift in the direction of practical strategies to support living languages to stay alive and thrive, or bring sleeping languages back to life. Linguistics needs to move to an interdisciplinary approach, incorporating fields such as applied linguistics that identify, investigate and offer solutions to real-life problems in communities and combine this with other fields, such as descriptive linguistics.

Can we imagine documenting a master–apprentice program or language nest for example? These programs can be conducted in language revival situations also. I can imagine several PhD or MA research projects happening in one language site.

This would see a new paradigm in linguistics in the Australian context. However, currently there are barriers to seeing this actualised. These barriers generally have very little to do with the non-Indigenous linguist's genuine desire to help Indigenous communities urgently save their languages from going to sleep, or breathing life back into them. The barrier is in fact the research funding model.

5.7 Research funding

Major research funding bodies, such as the Australian Research Council and universities, have a very narrow view of 'research' and currently do not support language maintenance or revival activities. These types of activities are funded by a different government organisation that supports the type of practical language activities described above and more, such as the operational costs of language centres.

However, this funding is very small compared to research funding and is dependent on the government of the day and that party's idiosyncratic support for Indigenous languages. In the past several years, we have seen major cuts to the Indigenous budget, leaving language centres all but crippled, with very little support for language maintenance or revival.

We are already beginning to see a shift in research funding in the requirement to demonstrate that research outcomes are more applicable to Indigenous communities on the ground. Again, can we imagine language maintenance and revival activities as linguistic research sites? Can the field of linguistics lobby research funding agencies to recognise these activities as valid and crucial research sites that also support language maintenance and revival?

Critically, it is now imperative for non-Indigenous linguists to begin to align their research to the agendas of Indigenous people. Before too long there will be no living Aboriginal languages left to study in Australia, as non-Indigenous linguists themselves keep telling us.

Further, with Indigenous communities beginning to reject linguistic research in some areas and some Indigenous organisations becoming anti-linguist, the situation is likely to get worse until Indigenous peoples' concerns are taken seriously and acted upon. Critically, then, non-Indigenous linguists must continue to lobby for change within the academy and funding bodies to bring research practice into line with the human rights of Indigenous people.

5.8 Appropriate training for non-Indigenous linguists

Many graduate non-Indigenous linguists go out into Indigenous communities with little or no understanding of the issues. They do much continued damage to the Indigenous communities in which they work, and they do much continued damage to the field of linguistics regardless of their best intentions.

It is of genuine ongoing concern that linguists get no formal training around the ethics of working with Indigenous communities and that the fieldwork courses that are offered (and there are not many in Australian universities) do not go anywhere near to addressing the issues from an Indigenous perspective. The same can be said for the majority of linguistics fieldwork guides, with the exception of just a couple.

This is a very unfortunate situation because it continues to perpetuate and compound all of the issues put forward in this book, and there is no hope for a deep understanding of the issues and change. It is therefore critical that undergraduates of linguistics—Indigenous and non-Indigenous—undertake some targeted in-depth training around the ethics of research and working with Indigenous communities if they intend to work on Indigenous Australian languages.

Such a course would need to be developed by Indigenous people. I have previously suggested that this could potentially be in the form of an online course developed in conjunction with and run out of AIATSIS, and that such a course could be a mandatory component of the ethics review process for working in Indigenous communities at all Australian universities.

As previously mentioned, in 2021 an online study group was formed called 'Decolonising Linguistics: Spinning a Better Yarn'. This study group offers insights into some of the issues outlined in this book and is open to anyone willing to learn.

Indigenous and non-Indigenous linguists can also take advantage of opportunities to work directly in Indigenous communities, such as an internship with Living Languages (formerly RNLD) or a language centre. Negotiating to volunteer at a language centre would better prepare young graduates for a career working with Indigenous Australian languages and give them some valuable on the ground training.

5.9 A new direction for collaboration

The steps to reform outlined in this book represent an incredibly positive move for the future of linguistics in Australia, as they are steeped in a human rights agenda that we can all feel good about. It might take some time to achieve, but it is, and will be, worth the effort we all make in the present.

Indigenous people have rightly pushed back against linguistic and other research that constitutes a breach of their human rights and will continue to do so until we see the changes we need. This could mean further restrictions on research in a variety of ways, including materials in archives and libraries, and this is already being realised.

However, this is a pendulum swing, and it will right itself when Indigenous people can see real change in linguistic practice that sees Indigenous people themselves as the authorities and protectors of their language and cultural knowledges again. Indigenous people need to be able to genuinely trust non-Indigenous linguists to be able to enter into genuinely collaborative research relationships that do not threaten this authority but, instead, deeply respect it in every regard.

But we need to come together and have those conversations about what this might look like on both sides. It is recommended that interested Indigenous linguists, language workers and language activists with a deeper understanding of the issues, and non-Indigenous linguists with a genuine desire to see change in the field of linguistics, come together at a forum to discuss and workshop the issues with a view to finding equitable and practical ways of moving forward together. However, we need to have those discussion within our respective communities first in order to be able to come to the table with clearly thought through and constructive positions.

This would be the most logical next step to gaining broad-ranging consultation and consensus on both sides and developing recommendations that would assist in bringing about long-needed reform around ethics in linguistic practice and research. We cannot wait another 30 years.

It is in this way that we will be able to genuinely collaborate, and this is the key to achieving all of our goals. Indigenous people can have their research agendas met and non-Indigenous linguists can have their research agendas met. They don't necessarily have to have the same goals, but the goals must be deeply understood and agreed to on both sides. We can turn the tide of linguistic and all research, from being seen as a tool of colonisation, to being seen as a part of an important strategy in Indigenous peoples' agenda in the continuing struggle for basic human rights and self-determination.

References

AIATSIS (Australian Institute of Aboriginal and Torres Strait Islander Studies). (2020a). *AIATSIS Code of Ethics for Aboriginal and Torres Strait Islander research*. Canberra: Australian Institute of Aboriginal and Torres Strait Islander Studies. aiatsis.gov.au/sites/default/files/2020-10/aiatsis-code-ethics.pdf

AIATSIS (Australian Institute of Aboriginal and Torres Strait Islander Studies). (2020b). *A guide to applying the AIATSIS Code of Ethics for Aboriginal and Torres Strait Islander research*. Canberra: Australian Institute of Aboriginal and Torres Strait Islander Studies. aiatsis.gov.au/sites/default/files/2020-10/aiatsis-guide-applying-code-ethics_0.pdf

AIATSIS (Australian Institute of Aboriginal and Torres Strait Islander Studies). (2012). *Guidelines for ethical research in Australian Indigenous studies. 2012*. Canberra: Australian Institute of Aboriginal and Torres Strait Islander Studies.

Angelo, Denise & Susan Poetsch. (2019). From the ground up: How Aboriginal languages teachers design school-based programs in their local language ecology, with Carmel Ryan, Marmingee Hand, Nathan Schrieber and Michael Jarrett. *Babel, 54*(1/2), 11–20. afmlta.asn.au/babel/

APFNHRI & OHCHR (Asia Pacific Forum of National Human Rights Institutions and the Office of the United Nations High Commissioner for Human Rights). (2013). *The United Nations Declaration on the Rights of Indigenous Peoples: A manual for national human rights institutions*. Sydney and Geneva: Asia Pacific Forum of National Human Rights Institutions and the Office of the United Nations High Commissioner for Human Rights. www.ohchr.org/sites/default/files/Documents/Issues/IPeoples/UNDRIPManualForNHRIs.pdf

Battiste, Marie. (2008). *Research ethics for protecting Indigenous knowledge and heritage: Institutional and researcher responsibilities*. In N. K. Denzin, Y. S. Lincoln & L. T. Smith (Eds), *Handbook of critical and indigenous methodologies*. Sage Publications Inc. doi.org/10.4135/9781483385686

Bell, Jeannie. (2003). *A sketch grammar of the Badjala language of Gari (Fraser Island)*. MA Thesis. Linguistics, University of Melbourne.

Bell, Jeannie. (2010). Language and linguistic knowledge: A cultural treasure. *Ngoonjook: Journal of Australian Indigenous Issues, 35*, 84–96.

Black, Paul & Gavan Breen. (2001). The school of Australian linguistics. *Forty years on: Ken Hale and Australian languages* (pp. 161–178). Canberra: Pacific Linguistics. hdl.handle.net/1885/254018

Bowern, Claire. (2015). *Linguistic fieldwork: A practical guide*: Springer. doi.org/10.1057/9781137340801

Bucholtz, Mary. (2019). Sociolinguistics trying to make a difference: Race, research, and linguistic activism 1. In Renee Blake & Isabelle Buchstaller (Eds), *The Routledge companion to the work of John R. Rickford* (pp. 242–250). New York: Routledge. doi.org/10.4324/9780429427886-25

Charity Hudley, Anne H. (2013). Sociolinguistics and social activism. In Robert Bayley, Richard Cameron & Ceil Lucas (Eds), *The Oxford handbook of sociolinguistics* (pp. 812–831). New York: Oxford University Press. doi.org/10.1093/oxfordhb/9780199744084.013.0040

Charity Hudley, Anne H., Christine Mallinson & Mary Bucholtz. (2019). Toward racial justice in linguistics: Interdisciplinary insights into theorizing race in the discipline and diversifying the profession. *Language, 96*(4) *Perspectives*. e200–e235. doi.org/10.1353/lan.2020.0074

Corris, Miriam, Christopher Manning, Susan Poetsch & Jane Simpson. (2004). How useful and usable are dictionaries for speakers of Australian Indigenous languages? *International Journal of Lexicography, 17*(1), 33–68. doi.org/10.1093/ijl/17.1.33

Couzens, Vicki. (2017). *Possum skin cloak story reconnecting communities and culture: Telling the story of possum skin cloaks Kooramookyan-an Yakeeneeyt-an Kooweekoowee-yan*. PhD Thesis. RMIT University. researchrepository.rmit.edu.au/esploro/outputs/doctoral/Possum-skin-cloak-story-reconnecting-communities/9921864010701341

Couzens, Vicki, Alice Gaby & Tonya Stebbins. (2020). Standardise this! Prescriptivism and resistance to standardization in language revitalization. In Keith Allan (Ed.), *Dynamics of language changes* (pp. 37–55). Springer. doi.org/10.1007/978-981-15-6430-7_3

Czaykowska-Higgins, Ewa. (2009). Research models, Community engagement, and linguistic fieldwork: Reflections on working within Canadian Indigenous communities. *Language Documentation & Conservation, 3*(1), 182–215.

Daes, Erica-Irene. (1993). *Study on the protection of the cultural and intellectual property of indigenous peoples [Special Rapporteur of the Sub-Commission on Prevention of Discrimination and Protection of Minorities and Chairperson of the Working Group on Indigenous Populations]*. Geneva: United Nations. www.refworld.org/docid/3b00f4380.html

Daley, Paul. (2021, 21 July). The plan to bury Mungo Man and Mungo Lady pains some traditional owners – and the man who found them. *The Guardian*. www.theguardian.com/australia-news/2021/jul/24/the-plan-to-bury-mungo-man-and-mungo-lady-pains-some-traditional-owners-and-the-man-who-found-them

Davis, Jenny L. (2017). Resisting rhetorics of language endangerment: Reclamation through Indigenous language survivance. *Language Documentation and Description, 14*, 37–58. www.elpublishing.org/PID/151

Denzin, Norman K., Yvonna S. Lincoln & Linda Tuhiwai Smith. (2008). *Handbook of critical and indigenous methodologies*: Sage Publications. doi.org/10.4135/9781483385686

DITRC (Department of Infrastructure, Transport, Regional Development and Communications), Australian Institute of Aboriginal and Torres Strait Islander Studies (Jacqueline Battin, Jason Lee, Douglas Marmion, Rhonda Smith & Tandee Wang), The Australian National University (Yonatan Dinku, Janet Hunt, Francis Markham, Denise Angelo, Emma Browne, Inge Kral, Carmel O'Shannessy, Jane Simpson & Hilary Smith). 2020. *National Indigenous Languages Report (NILR)*. Canberra: Department of Infrastructure, Transport, Regional Development and Communications, formerly the Department of Communications and the Arts.

Donaldson, Tamsin. (1985). From speaking Ngiyampaa to speaking English. *Aboriginal History, 9*(1/2), 126–147. doi.org/10.22459/ah.09.2011.07

Eira, Christina. (2000). *Discourses of standardization: Case study - the Hmong in the west*. PhD Thesis. Department of Linguistics and Applied Linguistics, University of Melbourne. minerva-access.unimelb.edu.au/handle/11343/39378

Eira, Christina. (2007). Addressing the ground of language endangerment. In Maya David, Nicholas Ostler & Caesar Dealwis (Eds), *Working together for endangered languages: Research challenges and social impact*, Conference, Foundation for Endangered Languages XI, 82–98. www.ogmios.org/conferences/2007/proceed2007.htm

Fesl, Eve D. (1993). *Conned!* St Lucia, Qld: University of Queensland Press.

Florey, Margaret Jean. (1990). *Language shift: Changing patterns of language allegiance in Western Seram*. PhD Thesis. University of Hawai'i at Manoa. hdl.handle.net/10125/9934

Gaby, Alice & Lesley Woods. (2020). Toward linguistic justice for Indigenous people: A response to Charity Hudley, Mallinson, & Bucholtz. *Language, 96*(4), e268–e280. doi.org/10.1353/lan.2020.0078

Gale, Mary-Anne. (2011). Rekindling warm embers: Teaching Aboriginal languages in the tertiary sector. *Australian Review of Applied Linguistics, 34*(3), 280–296. doi.org/10.1075/aral.34.3.02gal

Grounds, Richard. (2007). Documentation or implementation. *Cultural Survival Quarterly, 31*(2), 28. www.culturalsurvival.org/publications/cultural-survival-quarterly/documentation-or-implementation

Hale, Kenneth. (1972). Some questions about anthropological linguistics: The role of native knowledge. In Dell Hymes (Ed.), *Reinventing anthropology* (pp. 382–397). Pantheon Books.

Hector, Ivy Kulngari, Jungurra Kalabidi, George, Banjo, Spider, Nangari Ngarnjal Dodd, Topsy, Jangala Wirrba Wavehill, Ronnie, Danbayarri, Dandy, Nanaku Wadrill, Violet, Puntiyarri, Bernard, Bernard Malyik, Ida, Wavehill, Biddy, Morris, Helen, Campbell, Lauren, Meakins, Felicity & Wightman, Glenn. (2012). *Bilinarra, Gurindji and Malngin plants and animals: Aboriginal knowledge of flora and fauna from Judbarra/Gregory National Park, Nijburru, Kalkarindji and Daguragu, Northern Australia*. Katherine Northern Territory Bilinarra, Gurindji and Malngin People; Department of Land Resource Management.

Henderson, John & Veronica Dobson. (1994). *Eastern and central Arrernte to English dictionary*. Alice Springs: IAD Press.

Hill, Clair & Patrick McConvell. (2010). Emergency language documentation teams: The Cape York Peninsula experience. In Hobson, John, Kevin Lowe, Susan Poetsch & Michael Walsh (Eds), *Re-awakening languages: Theory and practice in the revitalisation of Australia's Indigenous languages* (pp. 418–432). Sydney: Sydney University Press. hdl.handle.net/2123/6918

Hinton, Leanne. (2010). Language revitalization in North America and the new direction of linguistics. *Transforming Anthropology, 18*(1), 35–41. doi.org/10.1111/j.1548-7466.2010.01068.x

Hinton, Leanne (Ed.). (2013). *Bringing our languages home: Language revitalization for families*. Berkley: Heyday. ORIM.

Hinton, Leanne & Ken Hale (Eds). (2001). *The green book of language revitalization in practice.* New York: Academic Press. brill.com/view/title/24315. doi.org/10.1017/s0047404502284055

Hinton, Leanne, Leena Huss & Gerald Roche. (2018). *The Routledge handbook of language revitalization.* New York: Routledge. doi.org/10.4324/9781315561271

Hobson, John, Kevin Lowe, Susan Poetsch & Michael Walsh (Eds). (2010). *Re-awakening languages: Theory and practice in the revitalisation of Australia's Indigenous languages.* Sydney: Sydney University Press. hdl.handle.net/2123/7888

Hokowhitu, Brendan, Aileen Moreton-Robinson, Linda Tuhiwai-Smith, Chris Andersen & Steve Larkin. (2020). *Routledge handbook of critical Indigenous studies.* London: Routledge. doi.org/10.4324/9780429440229

Hudson, Joyce & Patrick McConvell. (1984). *Keeping language strong: Report of the pilot study for the Kimberley Language Resource Centre.* Broome: Kimberley Language and Resource Centre.

Jacobsen, Britt. (2018). *Language documentation and community-empowering projects: Bridging the gap.* University of Sydney MA Thesis.

Janke, Terri. (2009). *Writing up Indigenous research: Authorship, copyright and Indigenous knowledge systems.* 4b0a135d-0afc-4211-ad92-391c5def66bb.filesusr.com/ugd/7bf9b4_a05f0ce9808346daa4601f975b652f0b.pdf

Janke, Terri. (2021). *True tracks: Respecting Indigenous knowledge and culture.* Sydney: NewSouth Publishing. www.newsouthbooks.com.au/books/true-tracks/

KLRC (Kimberley Language Resource Centre). (2010). Whose language centre is it anyway? In Hobson, John, Kevin Lowe, Susan Poetsch & Michael Walsh (Eds), *Re-awakening languages: Theory and practice in the revitalisation of Australia's Indigenous languages* (pp.131–145). Sydney: Sydney University Press. hdl.handle.net/2123/6930

Leonard, Wesley. (2017). Producing language reclamation by decolonising 'language'. *Language Documentation & Description, 14,* 15–36. www.elpublishing.org/docs/1/14/ldd14_02.pdf

Leonard, Wesley. (2021). Centering Indigenous ways of knowing in collaborative language work. In L. Crowshoe, I. Genee, M. Peddle, J. Smith, C. Snoek (Eds), *Sustaining Indigenous languages: Connecting communities, teachers, and scholars* (pp. 21–34). Arizona: Northern Arizona University. jan.ucc.nau.edu/~jar/SILL/SILL3.pdf

Little, Carol-Rose, Travis Wysote, Elise McClay & Jessica Coon. (2015). Language research and revitalization through a community-university partnership: The Mi'gmaq research partnership. *Language Documentation & Conservation, 9*, 292–306. hdl.handle.net/10125/24644

Mahboob, Ahmar, Britt Jacobsen, Melissa Kemble & Zichen Catherine Xu. (2017). Money for language: Indigenous language funding in Australia. *Current Issues in Language Planning, 18*(4), 422–441. doi.org/10.1080/14664208.2017.1331497

Meakins, Felicity. (2008). *Case-marking in contact: The development and function of case morphology in Gurindji Kriol, an Australian mixed language.* PhD Thesis. Department of Linguistics and Applied Linguistics, University of Melbourne. hdl.handle.net/11343/39332

Meakins, Felicity, Jennifer Green & Myfany Turpin. (2018). *Understanding linguistic fieldwork.* London: Routledge. doi.org/10.4324/9780203701294

Meakins, Felicity & Patrick McConvell. (2021). *A grammar of Gurindji: As spoken by Violet Wadrill, Ronnie Wavehill, Dandy Danbayarri, Biddy Wavehill, Topsy Dodd Ngarnjal, Long Johnny Kijngayarri, Banjo Ryan, Pincher Nyurrmiari and Blanche Bulngari.* Berlin: Mouton de Gruyter. doi.org/10.1515/9783110746884

Meakins, Felicity, Xia Hua, Cassandra Algy & Lindell Bromham. (2019). *Birth of a contact language did not favor simplification. Language, 95*(2), 294–332. doi.org/10.1353/lan.2019.0032

Miller, Robert L. & Richard Grounds. (2021). The legacy of hunter-gatherers at the American Philosophical Society Frank G. Speck, James M. Crawford, and revitalizing the Yuchi language. In Adrianna Link, Abigail Shelton and Patrick Spero (Eds), *Indigenous languages and the promise of archives* (pp. 63–98). Lincoln: University of Nebraska Press. doi.org/10.2307/j.ctv1k03s31.9

Mirima Dawang Woorlab-gerring Language and Culture Centre and Knut J. Olawsky & Frances Kofod. (2019). *Miriwoong Woorlang Yawoorroonga-Woorr: A Miriwoong Lexicon for All* (2nd ed). Kununurra: Mirima Council.

Musgrave, Simon & Nicholas Thieberger. (2007). Who pays the piper? In Maya David, Nicholas Ostler, Caesar Dealwis (Eds), *Working together for endangered languages: Research challenges and social impact,* Conference, Foundation for Endangered Languages XI. www.ogmios.org/conferences/2007/proceed2007.htm

Nakata, Martin N. (2007). *Disciplining the savages, savaging the disciplines.* Canberra: Aboriginal Studies Press. aiatsis.gov.au/publication/35550

Newry, David & Keeley Palmer. (2003). Whose language is it anyway? Rights to restrict access to endangered languages: A North-East Kimberley example. In *Maintaining the links: Language, identity and the land: Proceedings of the Seventh Foundation for Endangered Languages Conference, Broome, WA* (pp. 101–06).

Office for the Arts. (2022). More than $57 million will be shared across 84 community-based Indigenous languages and arts activities. (28 July 2022). www.arts.gov.au/news/funding-indigenous-languages-and-arts-projects

Olawsky, Knut J. (2010). Going public with language: Involving the wider community in language revitalisation. In Hobson, John, Kevin Lowe, Susan Poetsch & Michael Walsh (Eds), *Re-awakening languages: Theory and practice in the revitalisation of Australia's Indigenous languages* (pp. 75–83). Sydney: Sydney University Press. hdl.handle.net/2123/6940

Pascoe, Bruce. (2014). *Dark emu: Black seeds: Agriculture or accident?* Broome: Magabala Books. www.magabala.com/products/dark-emu

Paton, Paul & Christina Eira. (n.d.). *Peetyawan Weeyn. A guide for community language programs*. Victorian Aboriginal Corporation for Languages. www.vacl.org.au/wp-content/uploads/2021/12/peetyawan-weeyn-brochure.pdf

Pérez González, Jaime. (2021). Ethical principles in linguistic fieldwork methodologies – According to whom? *Language Documentation & Conservation. Theoretical reflections around the role of fieldwork in linguistics and linguistic anthropology: Contributions of Indigenous researchers from southern Mexico* (Special Publication No. 23), 131–152. nflrc.hawaii.edu/ldc/sp23

Poetsch, Susan, Michael, Jarrett & Denise Angelo. (2019). Learning and teaching Gumbaynggirr through story: Behind the scenes of professional learning workshops for teachers of an Aboriginal language. *Language Documentation & Conservation, 13*, 231–252. hdl.handle.net/10125/24867

Raymond, Pompey Dakamajbi, Pharlap Dilkbarri Dixon, Sue 'Lady' Mangkanjangiwarra Dixon, Shannon Kulngankarri Dixon, Ray Dimakarri Dixon, Jeffrey Manawurda Dixon, Janey Walanyku Lunjabirni Dixon, Elizabeth Dixon, Mark Murrulunginji Raymond, Harold Injimadi Dalywaters, Jumbo Kijilikarri Collins, Robin Yikalamba Woods, Eileen Minyminyngali Peterson-Cooper, Felicity Meakins, Rob Pensalfini & Glenn Wightman. (2018). *Jingulu and Mudburra plants and animals: Biocultural knowledge of the Jingili and Mudburra people of Murranji, Marlinja, Warranganku (Beetaloo) and Kulumindini (Elliott) Northern Territory, Australia* Tennant Creek, NT/Batchelor, NT/Palmerston, NT: Papulu Apparr-Kari Aboriginal Corporation & Batchelor Institute Press & Department of Environment and Natural Resources. batchelorpress.com/node/380

Rice, Keren. (2009). Must there be two solitudes? Language activists and linguists working together. jan.ucc.nau.edu/~jar/ILR/ILR-4.pdf

Rickford, John R. (1997). Unequal partnership: Sociolinguistics and the African American speech community. *Language in Society, 26*(2). 161–197. doi.org/10.1017/s0047404500020893

Rigney, Lester-Irabinna. (1999). Internationalization of an Indigenous anticolonial cultural critique of research methodologies: A guide to Indigenist research methodology and its principles. *Wicazo Sa Review, 14*(2), 109–121. doi.org/10.2307/1409555

Rigney, Lester-Irabinna. (2001). A first perspective of Indigenous Australian participation in science: Framing Indigenous research towards Indigenous Australian intellectual sovereignty. *Kaurna Higher Education Journal, 7*, 1–13. researchnow.flinders.edu.au/en/publications/a-first-perspective-of-indigenous-australian-participation-in-sci

Riley, Lynette. (2021). Community-led research through an Aboriginal lens. In V. Rawlings, J. Flexner & L. Riley (Eds), *Community-Led: Research: Walking new pathways together* (pp. 9–37). Sydney: Sydney University Press. doi.org/10.30722/sup.9781743327579

Said, Edward. (1978). *Orientalism*. New York: Vintage.

Smith, Linda Tuhiwai. (1999). *Decolonizing methodologies: Research and Indigenous peoples*. London UK: Zed Books.

Smith, Linda Tuhiwai. (2005). *On tricky ground: Researching the native in the age of uncertainty*. California: Sage Publications.

Stebbins, Tonya N. (2001). Emergent spelling patterns in Sm'algyax (Tsimshian, British Columbia). *Written Language & Literacy, 4*(2), 163–194. doi.org/10.1075/wll.4.2.03ste

Stebbins, Tonya N., Kris Eira & Vicki L. Couzens. (2017). *Living languages and new approaches to language revitalisation research*. New York: Routledge. doi.org/10.4324/9781315269078

Tasmanian Aboriginal Centre. (2021). *Palawa kani, the only Aboriginal language in lutruwita today*. tacinc.com.au/programs/palawa-kani/

Thieberger, Nick & Caroline Jones. (2017). *Indigenous linguistic & cultural heritage ethics policy*. ARC Centre of Excellence for the Dynamics of Language (updated 2021). legacy.dynamicsoflanguage.edu.au

Treloyn, Sally & Rona Googninda Charles. (2014). How do you feel about squeezing oranges? Dialogues about difference and discomfort in intercultural ethnomusicological research collaboration in the Kimberley. In Katelyn Barney (Ed.) *Collaborative Ethnomusicology: New Approaches to Music Research between Indigenous and Non-Indigenous Australians* (pp. 169–186). Melbourne: Lyrebird Press.

Troy, Jakelin. (1994). *Melaleuka: A history and description of New South Wales Pidgin*. PhD Thesis. Australian National University. hdl.handle.net/1885/112648

van Driem, George. (2016). Endangered language research and the moral depravity of ethics protocols. *Language Documentation & Conservation, 10*, 243–252. hdl.handle.net/10125/24693

Wadrill, Violet, Biddy Yamawurr Wavehill & Felicity Meakins. (2015). *Kawarla: How to make a coolamon*. Batchelor, Australia: Batchelor Press. batchelorpress.com/node/292

Wadrill, Violet, Biddy Yamawurr Wavehill, Topsy Ngarnjal Dodd & Felicity Meakins. (2019). *Karu: Growing up Gurindji*. Melbourne: Spinifex Press. www.spinifexpress.com.au/shop/p/9781925581836

Westerway, Michael, Doug Williams & Jason Kelly. (2021, 4 August). Mungo ancestral remains reburial proposal disrespects the Elders' original vision. *The Conversation*. theconversation.com/mungo-ancestral-remains-reburial-proposal-disrespects-the-elders-original-vision-164854

Wilkins, David. (1992). Linguistic research under Aboriginal control: A personal account of fieldwork in central Australia. *Australian Journal of Linguistics, 12*(1), 171–200. doi.org/10.1080/07268609208599475

Williams, Raymond. (1983). *Culture and society, 1780–1950*. New York: Columbia University Press.

Wilson, Shawn. (2008). *Research is ceremony: Indigenous research methods*. Halifax: Fernwood Publishing. fernwoodpublishing.ca/book/research-is-ceremony-shawn-wilson

Yamada, Racquel-Maria. (2007). Collaborative linguistic fieldwork: Practical application of the empowerment model. *Language Documentation & Conservation, 1*(2). hdl.handle.net/10125/1717